Ley Lines to Elsewhere

Alabaster & Mercury, Volume 2

Alabaster & Mercury
Ocean Beach, California

Kuechlin, Larry for
Chris Madoch, Kushal Poddar, Dwayne St.
Romain, Kimalisa Kaczinski, James Crafford,
Caili Wilk and Dan-Paul Flores (artist)
Ley Lines to Elsewhere, Alabaster & Mercury Vol. 2 p. cm
ISBN-13: 978-0982259108 (paper : alk. paper)
ISBN-10: 0982259107 (paper : alk. paper)

Copyright © 2014 by Larry L. Kuechlin, Jr.

First Edition.

All rights reserved. Printed in the United States of America. No part of this book may be used or reproduced in any manner whatsoever without the express written permission except in the case of brief quotations embodied in critical articles and reviews.

Published by:
Alabaster & Mercury
Ocean Beach (San Diego)
California, USA

Many of these poems were previously published in periodicals.

Dedication

This is the second volume of poetry that I have crafted for Alabaster & Mercury, and I do believe that I may have it right this time. Each of these exceptional Poets are here to offer you a book of their own within this book. I have left, as much as I could, their content and order to the Poets themselves, and kept my editorial voice out of the equation. The result, I believe, is an amazing look into poetry itself and all the facets that we spend so long pondering, pontificating and arguing over.

I am truly honored to have been a part of this in any sense, but to have so many wonderful Poets entrust me with their work is something that I will carry with me through the darkness and the light.

I want to thank, in particular, Chris Madoch who embraced this project from the beginning, and through the long delays from health issues and matters of life that could not be avoided, he kept his faith and friendship firmly with me.

Larry Kuechlin
Publisher, Alabaster & Mercury

For Chris Madoch

Contents

03: Dedication
04: Contents

Chris Madoch
10: Calendar Wars
11: the Empty Dish
12: Found Hours
13: Wisdom That No-One Would Tire of Hearing
14: Soul Traces
16: Cannibalism Is Back
17: Slip and Blood
18: Seven Seconds
20: The First of the Indian Summers
21: Nature Splitting Her Sides
22: The Passing of a Dog
23: Real and Virtual Dicks
24: Soundbites From the Hospital Café
26: The Waste of Words
27: As Complicated As It Gets
28: As Opposed to Prayer
29: Life Class

Kushal Poddar
36: Eternity Defined by a Cave
37: In the Unreal Black and White
38: Undead
39: After a Conversation With Her Husband
40: The Secret
41: The Praying Cricket
42: A Special Child
43: These Are Not-

44: A Sweet and Sour Tune
45: Local Marching Band
46: The God With the Plastic Bricks
47: We Move the Coming Years Towards Right
48: Mirrored Day
49: Tattoo
50: Knots, Mouldy
51: All Calm Underneath
55: Double Spaced
54: Basement of the War
56: The Shoes
57: Morning, Kolkata

Dwayne St. Romain

62: One Howl Winding
63: The Hummingbird Grill
66: A Psalm of Calm
67: The Day After
70: Midway
71: What Am I
74: The Fit
76: Dusk
78: Then
79: Funeral for a Fat Ass
82: Eavesdropping In Ghostland
84: Beside You
86: Rainbow Runner
88: My Place
90: the Mojo
92: The Pit of Lingers
93: Suraya

Kimalisa Kaczinski

98: Breathing Room
99: This Used to Be a Love Poem

100: Growing Crows
101: Always a Train
102: The Wish
103: Sleep
104: Growth
105: Lass
106: Motherhood
107: A Sky Turned Blue
108: American Girl
110: The Pacific Ocean
111: He Loves Me, He Loves Me Not
112: The Cool Side of the Bed
113: Crushed
114: Orion's Belt
115: Tess, as She Moves
116: The Night I Met Richard Gere
117: Husband Number Four
118: Lake Powell
120: Finding Poetry After the Mountains Have Gone Away
121: Snow
122: Let Us Go Then, You and I

James Crafford

126: The Nebulous Labyrinth
127: The Nebulous Labyrinth, pt. 2
128: Dirge On a Stormy Afternoon
129: A Shy God Hiding
130: Me and Circe Make a Go of It
131: The Microscopic Report
132: The Dagger of Neglect
133: Chrysalis
134: The Impermanence of Mothers
135: Within the Unseason

Caili Wilk
140: The invisible light
141: The light has changed
142: the feast
143: Asecular Spirituality
144: Honesty
145: The Mistake
146: Ice
148: Regret
150: after the party, in a grassy lot
151: Rites
152: Rainbows
153: Phenomena
154: California
155: Summer
156: Historical Materialism
158: Impact
159: Reminiscent

Larry Kuechlin
162: Departure From Shalford Rail Staition
166: Acrylic On Canvas
167: A Need for Broken Things
168: White
170: A Little Blood to Cover the Dark
171: Ice Skating
174: Essence
176: His Girl
178: 3 a.m. connections
180: Days Like These

Chris Madoch

Calendar Wars

That has passed- and that
So why be arsed with all the vying
Calendars
With claims to be the one that counts time
Unaccountably

Besides, inaccuracy dresses me in joy
Employing
Momentary momentousness
Then leaving, breathing on in love's continuum
Which I treasure
For its confounding impossibility to be
Quantified or measured by the fuss of us.

That last snowfall's all but melted dead.
It won't be back but another is expected- forecast,
Said: and it will be quite different of course,
White again;
No two snowflakes ever are the same;
Souls also.

Calendar wars spore
Copy-cats addicted to exactitude
Poor attitude, ingratitude.
They talk a good game
Play foul-
Walk away lame.

We fly between the finest raindrops
Across the void between one moment and the next-
Living.

The Empty Dish

Rest. Take a breath. Step back from life as you know it.
Too soon you will be leaving
mooning over why and grieving the lost
opportunities you tossed to one side, trod on, binned.
Let regret begin-

You eschewed love when you knew it to be true
and you chose greenhouse roses
traded truth for that charade of consequences
where pretence and airs and graces stuffed
the many empty places in your heart.

Dead. Dreadfully apart. A bridge too far.
You could try haunting him
and wish your spectral whispers
might just reach his child-like hearing.

The home he's in is full of others scorned by sense-
they sit in half circles shedding tears
gazing in wonder at day time television's
circus of unkindness.
At night they are drugged into a psychic blindness.

Now you are crying too. You always used to do this
when what you wished for proved to be an empty dish.

Found Hours

Lost moments ever plead for more time
to reveal their meaning-

you missed a daughter's first bleeding
a son's initial spilled seeding;
took the fear in their pubescent eyes
to suggest a dislike of the crickets sawing
or the wasps swarming.

Many such examples stack-up
in a life wasted for the want of watching out
for small things-

a boy's sudden attention to laundry
a girl's subtle change of head carriage.
The way death can so deftly
scythe through the wheat fields of a marriage.

You come to all three early graves
a widowed crone with weeping flowers
willing your lapses in memory to fill with found hours.

That patriarchal grey sky you cling to
spots your well thumbed bus time-table
sees you counting on your bony fingers.
He enables tears and the obligatory rain.

Wisdom That No-One Would Tire of Hearing

I strike a match- bright testimony
to our evolved inventiveness.
I then make the lips of this small flame
kiss the crinkly cellophane-
the wrapping of a small brick of accelerant
and wait
anticipating great chemistry
unfolding in my hearth like
minor 'miracles' are prone to do in man's hands:
and with the adding of slim timber and jet black coal,
with our arrogant belief in abilities to voodoo certainties,
I allow the process room and breath.

Turning off all the other lights, killing the electricity,
I sit and stare with some pale ghost of hope
at my lonely fire of lost community-
the dark being stippled by escaping energies,
a release of 3000 years of hidden sleep
from something made rock by the songs of time.

This is no 'divine' spark
but the bark of ancient tree ferns
giving up its petrified light.

My dogs make pillows of my slippered feet
and we all bask in this recovered heat
forged by the Sun that shone on history's child
when we believe our Earth was awful wild.

I begin to regret the loss of imagined gatherings
where, before sleep, the elders would repeat
their legacy of remembered tales
about the wonder of Mammoths and Blue Whales-
verbal wisdom that no-one would tire of hearing.

Soul Traces

We romanticise the prizes of our foolish speculations
accede to the temptations of invented mysteries
make the esoteric too deep to plumb, become in thrall
to all the occult nonsense that appeals to our base senses
always seeking pleasure in our flight from pain,
our adoration of sunshine, our frustrations with the rain-no
wonder we are inclined to deify the elfin random,
to summarily abandon sheer wonder in the presence of
all things wondrous that make our ignorance gleam thunderous.

The mass of team mankind collecting like some lame detritus
in morasses of our own making, blind to ever breaking slumber,
intoxicated by the meanest theories, drugged by sameness,
thwarted by every query as if they are the warts of black death.
Ego always dancing on the tongues of our self-centric minds,
we leave behind the sweet spots of our limitless potential
and all for some remorseless rot we label reverential.

You could waste a whole life embracing faith in the misunderstood
where no place of worship could replace the small magnificences
we incline to ignore in favour of flesh, blood: rice wafers and wine.

You could instead have seen it all, both the wood and the trees,
to have witnessed free-will playing 'It' with all the dancing leaves
alive with atmosphere and fearless of the heartbeats of the breeze.
You could have abandoned hope, the stresses of abandonment
and coped far better with the letter of all universal natural laws.
You could easily have settled your history of old scores with
science.

You should have shredded from your heads what faith embedded
there via vile phials of religion's endless store of long hypodermics.

Addictions to the fanciful have had the bulls of us castrated,
the cows given hysterectomies.
That is how captive our herd-species is to futility.

No doubt disquieting answers will eventually out.

In that disputed darkness prior to the Big-Bang-
that egg of void we all seek to avoid in fear of gods,
in terror of our characteristic choir of human errors,
some truth rang a bell or fired a starting gun.
Our great event could not have been the only one.

It is devilish perverse to think that ours is but a single universe
and I will not let this product of our arrogance disease me
or freeze me from all reasonable interaction with the here and now
where the only proven miracle is life itself and all nonsense besides
withers wet with lies, drowns in our clowning and finally is realized
upon the stainless steel where forensics force the ultimate reveal-
all soul traces gently placed inside a Petri dish as I would lovingly
wish.

Cannibalism Is Back

Avaricious misfits
some no more than genitals on sticks
have stolen the genuine
made them submit, raped their mystic gifts
and ridden into the coming dawn
like porn stars draped in seminal fluids-
they are pearlescent ghosts,
pale imitations of angels in harness to our dreams.

Tomorrow's stakes are high-
the proper poets tied atop the fire of young sparks
larking with passion as if it were an alcopop
their thirst made worse by misplaced ire
and an addiction for sugar,
brandish brands ablaze with grave misunderstandings.

The fat of all art history melts
makes crisp crackling of respect.
That fact haunts the future timeline
accompanied by smug markers planted by
rap, graffiti and crap wannabees.

Cannibalism is back.

Slip and Blood

Lashings of inclement wet-
the gutters spluttering unusual regret;
decorative maize leaves channelling the grief
of two hours of torment, lawns raped by nature.
The green shrieks of the drowning red ants
a moving sequence, one of many
in the day's disaster epic- 'Local Flooding'

I'd watched the anger of a four by four
disgorge a trapped cat.
Mindless magma does that to cold boulders-
melts granite in a split second.

Tsunamis rip potted plants from hotel balconies
deprive the native gardeners of their livings-
their lives, their wives' lives, the lives of their offspring.

Our lush West Sussex lane
is still awash with slip and blood.
Best stop crying. Regardless of the mundane facts
the Sun will soon reliably shine again.
Better to smile, be British and tut at the weather
than to flirt so publically with the sanity of madness.

Seven Seconds

two grey squirrels
dance
by chance describing
DNA spirals
on the lichen clad trunk
of a hazel nut tree

I silently bark
heel
to a pup of an opinion

crossing the orchard
crushing
fallen fruit underfoot
just as a soldier's boot would
the skull
of a winged bird
on its way out

lavender furniture polish
rained upon dogs
wind-blown bed linen
and a new brew
old strands of being British
losing ground

blue television news
all the blame made far more tame
by blonde bomb-shells

a screech of car brakes
the ache in the arse
survivor
berates the Asian driver with
you black bastard

impending sleep
files away all of the above
never a lost moment
each
waiting for recall
when push comes to shove

The First of the Indian Summers

Light blondes my dog in bars
he is the knowing one
now glowing as the sun reaches far inside
our bungalow
beset by this sudden raid of golden spears
its sofa shade so cruelly impaled
that I hold up a pillow in defence
and watch its silver threads catch fire
like thought, or some desire wrought
in the heat of moment.

It is stark contrast that has roused us
from a drowsiness with its menacing barking.
The clever Tibetan's moved into deeper daytime dark-
gives me a look that says grey clouds
are massing close by.
A counter-attack against this first
of the Indian Summers is
soon to be underway.

Nature Splitting Her Sides

A flabby pretty shabby air
lies lolling on the dimpled
thighs/skies of bruised cellulite:

excess baggage
of the fat whore Summer- grown obese
on over-egged-n-buttered trees and sex cheese,
ten trillion effusive seedings on the rob
of any means to reach a moist soil oven.

Breeding fever's peaked at full throb-
Laura Ashley visitors to my garden invariably speak of
beauty, beauteousness,
as they earnestly ogle insects, plants, birds, bees
on the job, unperturbed by plural prats
playing the part of this orgy's uninvited voyeurs
hiding their blushes under straw and voile hats.

Genius plants use all God's creatures for their own ends-
schmuck,
check the viable/friable earth stuck to your shoe;
next year's invasive thistles may have hitched a ride
to quantum leap a country mile across the city with you.
Not that prickles would be tolerated in Hampstead.
It is one of those London dead vicinities,
the wildlife having migrated to The Heath and Cemetery.

I like to think that nature splits her sides
at how we pretend we are,
scattering spit and laughter at our vast expense.
There is so much of us she obviously derides-
our poisonous love affair with the car,
the way we watch our violence in spin affected mirrors
and see, on reflection, only innocence.

The Passing of a Dog

Good-bye- [the diminished 'God be with you.']
would not ever do
just could not cut the mustard in the circumstance
of my old dog's final dance
with heart parts tripping out and fear gripping him for once;
his screams bleaching bright summer green
from the fresh mown lawn;
fifteen long years searing through his Tibetan scrawn
with all the lactic acid of a false dawn:
what were vets for? To perform pet miracles.

The dispensing of a 'clean pair of heels' dispatch.
But you'll still cry wire wool tears
that scratch your retinas; you'll bite your bottom lip
and let it let blood on your fawn silk shirt;
you'll set about burying the hurt in clipped speech.

Holding him [impeaching some delusional being]
you'll feel the intubated drug begin to sing-
it lures the blue-whale in him to a deathly beaching.
In some envy of this smooth transition
you'll dwell on your humanitarian position
when inevitably push will come to shove-
mercy killing is indubitably an instrument of love,
but you will have to howl out loud this case for you
and there are many who would quickly call you barking.

I chose a rosewood box for my dog's ashes
and have begun the clock-watching
waiting for the phone to say he's done-
put through the grinder and reduced to his minimum.
Time has since developed a serious cardiac condition
chimes on every quarter have found a random disorder;
there are whispers abroad of anarchy in heaven.

Real and Virtual Dicks

A dogged dog-eared canine name comes up
again, again
interrupting the way I sort my in-box
with delete delete-
the depth of his old deceit is easily refreshed
and I revisit a brief breathlessness
but all trace of former tenderness is in absentia now:
his writing still lacks the bravura and the balls.
A stench funnels from my memory's bowels-
his howling. How it still appals.

His vivid emails still exist-
the lurid details of his mind's perverse excursions
into the virtual impropriety of a married father
fancying he'd rather try a spell of being gay.
It was a queer way to run away from the bitter mess
and bitterness of his heterosexual reality.

Ruthless his prodigious denials-
I have a fat file of unapologetic retractions
proofs of broken promises and thefts.
Left is the idea that I might write our episode out-
one other fact-fucked fiction
in a whole collection littered with erections:
real and virtual dicks.
Maybe the time is right to edify the prick with something
appropriately comedic.

Soundbites From the Hospital Cafe

Holbein and Goya saw pictures in the embers
Of the ugly and the part dismembered
Dregs
Who had not the legs for marathons or pole-dancing:
It is a thread in art that tugged at Dianne Arbus' heart;
Made her shoot images on the edge of propriety,
Black and white sights
That challenged an American middle class
Palette sick of pastel piety.

The décor here is near to well-worn Eastern European.
St Richard's Chichester. Spot the Doctor, Vicar, Sister.

Your mother had another fall?
She did, yes.
Bless. Well how appalling. Anything broken?
Her spirit and her pelvis.
Maybe she'd appreciate a ward library token?
The way that you appeared..
Yes.
Could you disappear as easily.
I am an accredited volunteer.
Nevertheless. Your face is uninvited in my space.

There are the workers and those they work upon.
It is a process bereft of humane interaction.
Nurses fat as blood filled tics
Sampling blood from victims fat as blood filled tics-
The odd Jim thin, grinning in his jim jams
Away with the house-martins chasing thunder-flies.

You dying or trying?
Dying?
Me too- fifty years smoking thirty a day in the cab of a lorry.

So sorry.
Not me- seventy two but my lungs might as well be
One hundred and three. They're proper fucked.
Given up?
The stress would kill me.
You?
The big 'C' rectally.
Ew! Difficult to sit?
It's a bugger to shit- they gave me a bag.
Thought I caught a whiff. Sorry.
Doesn't bother me. Used to moving human waste all over the place.
Oh I get it- sespit tanker.
You got it wanker. No disgrace- there's always been money in muck.
Fuck yes.
Need your bag emptying.

No thanks. I was being neighbourly.
Thanks. I'm at that stage where I'm owning my own stoma.

We eat bacon and scrambled egg sandwiches-
Granary bread; sip from brown mugs of Cappuccinos;
Nothing much needs to be said;
The sights make such a stained glass sight for sore eyes
That a cathedral silence imposes itself like a cowl of faith.

Deep down in the bowels of my soul
Something vivid choosing life as opposed to God
Gives out a muted howl.

I will always, in all circumstances, elect to be stone dead
If ever I'm rendered useless by the systems you trust
Found to be not fit for purpose
Meat for a peep show or the circus;
Weathered into a gay man
unable to paint the nearest town red.

The Waste of Words

This grave edge of what we are about
defines a well
that is well worth the drinking from.
Mordernly we've become increasingly crap at death-
the thing that haunts our every living breath;
the thing we clownishly deny exists
until it stops our heart.

We flock at funerals like absurd birds
in rare plumage-
the feathers barely weathered, moth balled;
hung out in the sun,
and we call out in uncommon grief
as the thief of shared experiences makes good
his escape
with someone who meant something to us,
though now is not the time to tell them.
They would not appreciate the fuss
or the waste of words.

As Complicated As It Gets

Would it stretch credulity
To have us show some due humility
In the superior presence of plants-
To, at the very least, appraise that circumstance?

There are many holes in civilisation's roof.
I am often at a loss
To stay dry for my tears let alone
The poisonous precipitations that constantly appear.

The mass, pale imitators of the genuine us,
They are engaged
In a perpetual froth of disengagement;
On the run, escaping from their native apes within
That they have close shaved and clothed cleverly
In order to sit pat atop the stale order;
A damned chain of command
That they've insidiously constructed in the vain hope
That that day will come when what's been aped
Will be made hideously gospel
Taken by those easily taken in to be a universal truth.
Space-rats. The hum-drum snare drum drivel of dross-
It comes raping the sanctity of my silence regardless.

There has never been or ever will be the proof.

I don't get concrete, even when they've stained it green,
Made a patterned block screen of it; planted
Their mark like a new strain of drug-resistant STD
And said sweetly to the mugged climber- there you go,
You know the chances, grow or die. Honeysuckle. Ivy.

The sun rises, appears to fly across the sky then sets.
I'm certain I want this to be as complicated as it gets.

As Opposed to Prayer

Looking back
at that seeming endless track-
my caravan of aged pack animals,
I watch them shimmer in the far hot haze
distortions contorting in time's desert sun;
so long is this line
all of its constituent parts remain uncountable.

It is no estimate of my wealth
but some hum drum measure of my mental health-
unable to let go of untold sores, old scores,
far flung dung-heap disappointments;
the obsessed tapestries of torture and stitch-up cruelties
that walked into my life like smiling friends of Christ
then left, unfeelingly, revealed as proven enemies
of all things rational and real to me-
those damned cruel tools of our world of artifice edified,
fools who have deified what's not been there.

There is no psychology of kind forgetting,
no biology that finds regret abominable.

New-age 'moving on' is just an ugly transitory
pop-song
its dumb dee dumb message criminally wrong.

But yet, the taking of every thorn from my aching feet
might add a new spring to my lingering winter step.
I wince again, walking through my dwelling place in pain,
seeking in vain a pair of tweezers as opposed to prayer.

Life Class

You so froth at the mouth for it
Round the clock buffets of media bites
At your neck, your cheek with the teeth of rabid vermin-

......images [streams of porn] sworn to psychotic secrecy
......sounds [waves] drowning out your screaming privacy
......smells [swell] hells cheese a Stinking Bishop comestible
......words [current] lout about spouting nowt digestible

The hooded Corvidae of buy one get one free [BOGOF]
An advertising venom worming its way in via your veins
At pains to have complimented your demented vanity.

These are those days when the sane and the insane
Play the game of Identical Twins-
Hands on your heart can you tell them apart
Our shy Chinese masters?
[We grin, sin, bare our base desires;
A tissue of lies we'll all fall down.] It's you-
That twitch in the slightly slack left eye-lid
A dead giveaway: Prozac; Valium; Quetiapine.
Did you, as a child raised in rural Devon,
Pull the wings off of live flies ever, Meadow Blues?
Wild. Ever gut a breathing duck? Ever have a vision?
Lose your rag? Ever been abused by a fudge-packer dad?
Mad.
......Sad unfurling world of cut flowers past their best
......limp petals curled in pleas upon an editor's desk.
......Books as profuse as fleas alive with irritating diseases.
......Maybe the bees are bleeding, leaving.

Glued to our twittering till queues we confuse the free will
To spend on spending cash or cum with FREEDOM-
Escape from ever
Ending the glitter itch some bitch faggot dared to call addiction:

PUNTS; each new dalliance with the pleasure principle
Comes and goes like all those tabloid highs and lows that
You, in fact, have wagged your gilded fat cat fingers at;
Capitalist cunts;
No, 'no-life commodities' to be more blunt. So vulnerable
You are
To those with untold wealth who'll trip on power
Shower you with gifties, tease out with neat demonic stealth
Your inner beast who knows no actual boundaries
And rowdy crows it's found the ultimate sublime release
To
Please
Please itself-
Share a feast of fresh shit with brother/sister sufferers
To have your stiff dick explore whatever orifice
Pertly presents inviting lips sufficiently elastic

Gripping. All to cock. God Priapus the rock of ages
Still ejaculating from the messianic Marquis' pages
Writ in the Bastille.

As a rule all mankind's cruelties will fill the new curriculum.
Torture. Torture. More torture. Torture on tap.
Hogwarts' crap aborted- sluiced, processed,
sold on as mineral water.
Life class. Naked truth. Forensic proof. Play-school for Sadists
For rapists of species constantly conveying away.

No more buying. Payback. Crazy flagellant papacy. SAVE ME.
 [Bet. Bet you pray on your knees to win the Euro-Lottery]
WHAT WOULD YOU GIVE-
Your apple, your appalling all?
Humiliation? Intolerable sexual degradation? Dry crying?

Tongue-tied scant survivors either lie
Or commit suicide- birding absurdly from high windows
Their flight light as the palest black.
None rant. And, mostly, no-one says jack.

It's just not politick. This is us proper fucked
Misbelieving we are civilised and raising
That fragile false faith to some dumb implausible decorative art-
So now, only the extremities of the extreme
Delivers the forgotten dream of an unsullied path
Where something new might
Just have half a chance to start in unsoiled soil
With spring water dancing reels without chemicals
With understanding hands hands-on, green thumbed.
There are Poets versed in the esoteric properties of plants.

Nothingness and laughter- these words are key
Trust me.
Trust me not, selfish, self-contained, contented clot
Whose fear of CHANGE has made the rotting world deranged,
Made 'A Siberian Film' as necessary as the dispatch of
A genius in Ostia.
I'm resolved to calling it an unsolved war crime.

I'm also a queer, [Your beautiful out]
No worries then men's men:
You have nothing to fear from the tortured insights
Of the morally bankrupt, degenerate likes of me; for
How whole you are- the common norm,
From mouth-hole to arse-hole unswervingly tubiform.
Send me your death threats-
Bully bullied by the bully who was bullied too,
You know not what you do.
INGEST SHIT. Page three of 'The Sun' tabloid-
Some 'Tate Modern' priestess of The Goddess taunts,
Flaunting her paranoid plastic tits and bum.

You softly succumb to a Coke and a McDonald's- coochy choo;
Have a sneaky wank in the spic-n-span loo.
Hope's become a joke to you.

......My dog's bods like magnets to my heel
......we feel our way through frosted tines of green
......alive to being alive, alive to the unseen.

......The first of winter's snow-drops nods,
......in a chilly breeze at odds with bitter lemon sunlight,
......not in agreement with anything but colluding with nothing:
......its demonstrable lack of a predicament
......is
......a sight for sore eyes.

Chris Madoch writes in many genres and his Poetry is ever present in them all. Born of Welsh mining stock he has created a large internet footprint. His first collection of Poems is still in print- 'Rumours From The Balcony' and remains available to purchase from the publisher Erbacce's dedicated online sales site. Chris has long been the mentor of Poet Kushal Poddar- someone he considers one of the finest Indian Poets writing in English ever. He has undertaken to, once more, kick start an autobiography of a very long, diverse and troubled life titled "Letters to Kushal [in plain speak and conundrums]".

Kushal Poddar

Eternity Defined by a Cave

The intimate light has a small mouth
and through this stony intestine
one walks one hundred paces for it
but face to face it lacks the expected greatness-
I feel the cave God,
his rough coldness under my palm.

A loose muscled woman sleeps
with her mouth open.
From this end the darkness is eternity.

Inside I usually feel otherwise.

A bat flies off the pristine maw.
It has shared three cave minutes with me.
We have changed each other by some imprecise unit.

I savour her sweetness but sense my wavering.

In the Unreal Black and White

She taboos calling her.
His calls are distracting.

His middays are long;
his unsaid words,
now mounting the fence
after a circular chase on their lawn,
are his pastime.

She taboos him on her evenings;
they come in the damp verdant
with the options of lost and deep down.

His evenings are eggs
smelling proteins,
staleness, repetition.

He opens his pre-amputation album.
The photos are white-cornered
where the sticky tape ran.

The frames hold
the unreal black and whites.

Undead

An italicised sky,
speaks you are gone.

Death has tweaked me twice today.

Saved by grace.
is what you would have said
brushing the faith
and placing it
beside the other cluttered mantelpieces.

Unbroken remnant.

Now I believe in the formless.
Formlessness is my sprung daybed,
unmade in waiting for your noon hands.

The wind, the eider-down, the leaf fall-
coming from the window
blown like sun kissed dust motes
every cliché that I ever wrote is all italicised.

After a Conversation With Her Husband:

You write too much poetry.
She says her husband says.

On a triangular hanger
I suspend my shirt.

Repressed anger hides in my reply:
How do you express your heart?

She tells me:
I let you feed the insides of my cat:
Whenever he's away.

The Secret

After the fact
I go for a walk
circling the park-
a pond,
trees with couples
who have a pact.

Upon returning
I find you out-
sitting just like before.
'Come on, you resemble
a painting!' I shout.

'No' you whisper, 'I am dead.'

The Praying Cricket

The aloneness orchestra
finds a prodigious cricket bowing.

You open your one palm
and press it flat over the other- so.

There, God stands out-
not a petty cuss
but a cut-out mountain built
by the triangulation of your heart line
and head line.

Go. You climb up defying
your Hitchcock down the vertebrae
one rainy winter.
[The sudden blizzard has a downcast arrow
and the river is yet to give birth
to the silver fish.]

You never believed in everything before this.

A Special Child

The Special school fifth grader
reads my conversation
from the other pavement.

He smiles
and waves at me.
I snap the discussion shut.

We walk down the Friday side by side.
In his company
silence merely double-spaces the sentences-

and distance has no privacy.
I follow his talking fingers
detailing the day.

I do not ask him
if he heard the entire conversation
I had with his doctor over the phone.

These Are Not-

The organic walls of a prison

Ears make the prison walls
human, alive, fleshy with harking
ears.
I tell him how this reminds me of Dali.

He asks.
Did he live in a prison?

A fly watches us.
He says-
The word 'fly' has no bearing here.
They call them 'the eyes'.

So
the prison walls have eyes too.
What does this remind you of?
He stares at me.

I say.
Its all about the possibilities
eyes see but we ignore.

A bell rings.
The end of my visit?

He smiles.
It never happened.

A Sweet and Sour Tune

August end blooms in the piano farm.
The shadows tail her every room.
We listen to her house all day
and our father wheeled his father
towards a winter home.

The two houses stand in two different seasons.
Rain on our driveway
leaves a dissolving tire mark
we study all afternoon.
The neighbour's pianos tune up
together again.

Days later the grandfather clock
resumes a miraculous timekeeping.
Its hourly melody revives
the afternoon of downpour on this side of the hedge,
a pianoforte flowering on the other.

Local Marching Band

The trumpet knows the tuba's wife
whose first cousin plays the French horn,
and is engaged to the flute girl;
the tenor drum broke her first heart
and the cymbal banged her
out of three weeks deep depression.

A spiteful lady pours winter
upon this marching band.
We all know who caused the fox incident
in her one square meter of meagre poultry.
We do not discuss certain paltry things
but giggle warmly over a chilled beer.

The trumpet knows the tuba
through his wife's tales.
These tales have a nicotine taste
and in the middle of her telling of them
the power goes down.
The trumpet swears darkly
on the bad administration of power.

The wife lifts her bended wings.
Without the cloths they seem
to be quite the dressed chicken on a dirty plate.
On the couch the tuba reclines in his whiskeyed stupor.
A distant radio plays a mean blues saxophone,
the only instrument the local band lacks.

They still seek one.

The God With the Plastic Bricks

The child's plastic bricks
build the impossibilities of tricks.

The invasive ants gain poise
step by step.
Only they dare climb up to the buck level
where the top cornices mushroom.

The God of all these things,
has lost interest,
so instead sucks a toy-head.

I hate head sucking.
I say so.
Hate bodies waking up to a zombie sleep.

The child's parents make friends with me
thinking I know about the night erections.

Well, I can balance one pebble atop another
and leave them in space until they sparkle;
there they harvest their own halo
and stay waiting for the next eternity
when the moment of their birth becomes immaterial
and bottomlessness is rendered cold.

I say, I know only about sand castles.
The kid smiles.

I show him-
that in the folds leading to a paper boat
there also blooms a lotus.

Ha, ha, uncle.

The objects opposed to hate come together
and re-build life.

We Move the Coming Years Towards Right

The hotel has sea-turtle lampshades.
In the breeding season
sand near here turns olive with death
and the escaping small ones, making it big,
return to die the next year.

A turtle-shade bulb causes
a glow on your travel diary.
Yours is the mother, I say.
Mine is the child.
You close the daily record.
Let us sleep between the histories.

In dream we make up fresh truths.
They move towards the waves of our breath.

Over the morning Java we know-
we both saw blood. Blood.
We need the brighter white bulbs for night lamps,
I tell the manager.

When he says something about
the presence of all truths in whiteness
we both instantly decide-
for the coming year we shall be booking the resort
a few yards to the right from here.

Mirrored Day

This day feels too faint to hurt.
Tomorrow the wound will rise
from the middle of my earth

and I shall crack another mirror
for the mirrors smile
once we break the silver splinters wide.

Reflections carry
truths not even skin deep.
If these mirrors bleed,
I know I have a few more hours
before I wake up
and try the new day's cutting edge.

Tattoo

The heat from your tattoo
remains invisible,
glowing
mythic colour running down your neck.

I open your skin
and roll the insides out both ways,
gently,
as I had promised.

The sacred orange of the inner
becomes fluid,
moves its lost stillness;
heads towards your finger's blue tip

where it will be a lovelorn acid
that burns the city map on my nail.

I still keep touching your lips
waiting for some artist to sketch us
on a golden dome inside the stone godliness.

Knots, Mouldy

The knots remain,
not the hands that tied them,
not the entire railings,
not even half the house.

I chase the drying shadows
swinging open the sun.

The impalpable girls
circle the idle words
dancing in the middle.

The knots, black,
hard and soft,
rotten and permanent,
begin the invisible wires.
The birds sit on them.
The girls chase them away.

If I cut those knots
the world will fall in a heap of debris,
like autumn,
the brownish chrome,
bright but saddening to a degree.

All Calm Underneath

The white-out on the cemetery rocks
proves how long I've slept.
Snow holds a calm glow for a tropical man.

I envy the souls racked here
on their separate shelves-
they are aging for some proud collector.

A tree has lost its broad leaves.
I can walk easily upon them
or rest, breathless,
beneath their brittle blanket.

Double Spaced

Silence

double-spaces the words

between a father and a son.

The father has many synonyms for everything,

only one for the son.

Their yard

shortens the distance

to autumn.

The children rush through it.

Then they run back

leaving a trail of confetti.

Bach, the mother loved.

They do not play him anymore.

The father and the son,

They listen to the 'Bed of Roses'.

Silence

returns with the clouds.

Rain

closes the fissures.

Walls

ooze water.

Basement of the War

The brilliance on the one side,
blackness on the other,
the cellar lid stands in between.
My grandmother crosses this frontier.
The filament- still torn,
two stairs clear and the rest- shadows.

Not much to see either,
she keeps a hollow womb down there,
a belly,
the full hunger.

The things
she left on one side of the war
and picked up their imperfect replicas
on the other side
fill the upper stories,
the rooms we lived where she resided.

Her secret remains in the basement.
Hollow belly,
a womb without a seed,
full hunger.

She climbs down in autumn.
Cleans the room.
Our help costs her three bucks.
Then she closes the lid
upon the hollowness trailing her
up to the stair top and touching her heels.
Her week spot.

She kisses the lid down.

Her whisper brings up

the name of the only man
she did not find on this side of the war—
for real or mere imitation.

The Shoes

The new shoes,
used before
but not by her,
lift her above the cobbles, gums, snots, mud.

She watches
the road caving down
by three centimetres.
Clouds come three centimetres nearer.

The hair in her neck rises.
The fear she feels
knows nothing about immortality;
has no preparation for it.

And the infinity hangs around her
like a bubble.
She stands on those shoes' altars,
a god,
hoisted over the decaying city's veins.

New old shoes always show up
in the nearest dumpster-
she picked hers up hours ago.

Morning, Kolkata

From the basement of mist
the newspaperman arrives for the subscription.
His muffler carries the gray of last winter
his mother homemade it weeks before her death.

We know a lot about him.
This sometimes makes us feel good,
half human, a quarter God and at rest-
floating blue.

We offer him tea, the biscuits kept apart
for the other guests or whoever this phrase represents.

He lifts his tired feet and places them inside his mist.
They disappear with his polite body.

We have read no proper news in months.
I have this lactose intolerance and
cannot read anything too white.

You read the sports page and the comics.
I eat toast with some black tea headlines.

Whenever a bird flies from the roof of the mist
we think the newspaperman will return
with his corrigendum for solving our gastric syndromes.

Kushal Poddar :born in a warm corner of India, a lone child and brought up with his shadow mates, he began writing verses at the age of six. He adopted his second tongue as the language to dream on. Widely published in several countries, prestigious anthologies included Men In The Company of Women, Penn International MK etc and featured in various radio programs in Canada and USA and collaborated with photographers for an exhibition at Venice and with performers for several audio publications and above all mentored by Chris Madoch, he once answered in an Interview- "This morning a stranger from his seat next to mine in a public bus pointed out toward the sky, Does not the blue look like a child in a cradle? This is the role of poetry in our society. Poetry is a tool to arrest the vast beyond within the canvas of personal experience. To limit the limitless so our thirst and longing for it remains unquenched. And hence I write." He is presently living at Kolkata and writing poetry, fictions and scripts for short films when not engaged in his day job as a counsel/lawyer in the High Court At Calcutta. The forthcoming books are "Kafka Dreamed Of Paprika" and "A Place For Your Ghost Animals".

Dwayne St. Romain

One Howl Winding

Reposed and cocked from sprint to peak
Where timbered bluffs won't baffle shrill
A lupine cry twines through the sky
To catch Suraya like a kite

On zephyrs surf through gorge and hollow
Two thousand miles where rivers shallow
Beat echoes off of Grand Chenier
Beat tears from leaves like shattered glass

For scents and visions loud as time
The trial as bright as Fat Man's wink
But everywhere that you were there
Are wakes and eddies settling fast

I taste your blinding agony
That out sings all the cherubim
To stir with ghost where you have been
A nourishment of genesis

Still one howl winding on the wind
On comet's trial to close the pack
Relentless as a Nasgul's nose
Loves big as that first banging note

Two wolves since pups searched out in pain
Where whips and poisons fall like rain
Where peace still lives on mythic plane
One howl winding calls your name

The Hummingbird Grill

An orange shimmer listed like bent rusted ships
In wakes flipped off Camp Street
Where Lee sees o'er trees
And listens for Battle Hymns sung over Dixie

Once skid row; exploded in affluent commerce,
An upscale renewal paved clean
Lit and treed

Drawn there to stare at the red moon eclipsing
With tears boiling nerve endings
Broke, blank and drifting
Pass Emeril's, Le Chat Noir, the Howling Wolf's Den
To the Cab haunt of gut wads and fifty cent gin
Two dollars no holler for three over easy
With biscuits and grits and tits over fishnets
Absurd drunken Greeks after sinning with peasants
Share hustles with homeless and Artists and kin
The Humming Bird Bar and Grill's Hour Rate Inn

I set at a table. Formica and tin
Where cigarette smoke curled on chrome napkin bins
Like cat's tail in tender turn discerned my pity
My last twenty Christmas Eve
In a pitiless City

He turned, grinned and burped
Then a heavy set giggle and said "I am Rette"
With a wet breath in jiggers
"A drink for a poem or a cig for a listen?"
A good glance and flagged for the waitress
With whistle

"Rette needing Bourbon?" she looked at me faintly
Then quaintly succinctly she doctored my bill
And brought him a water glass filled till it spilled.

"Happy birthday Rette" nodded the waitress named Gladys

"Your Birthday?"

He shuddered with grand booming laughter
"Hell no but they're thinking and I'll take that gladly
And thinking of anyone else is soul soothing
Now truly a story?" He palmed chin and waited

"Mais then Rette you hungry before I begin?
You might lose the envy when I'm at the end
My ten year job down sized; a marriage long dead
My kids gone a thousand miles after all's said
Four months without money lost my family home
My grandparents built it on sweat without loans
I lost my last passion and hocked my guitar
A star crossed sad dreamer
Self cursed at the worst
Afraid of the dark; couldn't pay for the stone
Tired of the drink but can't leave it alone
I thought I belonged here but it's out my league
Intrigued by a loser? I'm the best I can be. "

He smiled with a twinkle and stroked his dark beard
And reached through his trench coat
For what was not clear
Then scratched deep near tearing for some sweet relief
Seriously the Bum said "Some parts I believe."
"My turn. A poem for a drink was the deal"

And spun tales of loss and of doom
Of fear and inadequate genius to live without beer
In words painting codex that restrung my mind
The kind of blind tune drop that syncs up the signs
He showed me that giving was all we could do
That what you lost hold on was just not for you
That pain simply tells one that something is broke
Joked "Its words were muted with very kind smoke
That stained as it scripted on Maple Leaf Rags
Then dragged out a handkerchief deep from his coat

He soaked up a spill that his whiskey had fed
Squeezed tight with his thumb then reached my forehead
With booze stinking thumb rubbed a spot that he'd seen
Closely inspecting said "Now you are clean"
"Go live for the giving and tell what you've seen
Your children still need you; You'll always have me.
Give of your last dollars like you bought this drink
And Think what you feel, never feel what you think."

"Hey wait" I lit up "I remember you now"
"But heard of you only, vagrant poet renowned
But had long ago died well I guess that's not true"
He smiled saying "Thirteen ways Possums see you"

I thanked him and walked out forgetting my bill,
Jerked wheeling, seeing the building condemned,
Boarded and brimmed with signs

"Condos In June;"
Walked the Maple Leaf Stride
Humming Scott Joplin tunes
Like a bird.

A Psalm of Calm

I never wander far away from you
Or test the true and blinding binding
Beneath our breathing
Your scalpel clean reveal
That steels through thicker things
We live behind
Delivers my reality
 To see singing signs in line

Can't cede my soul again;
Your pinnacle possession plated
So long ago now

Show me how
I'll throw a bigger fit,
A fill of cocoa comfort
Chills yield to,
Kisses granting wishes
Wilting lesser lessons
Building thistles into dandelions shrines
That brine fresh sun rays
Ricochet waves of mikveh warm wind in
And bend the light of love
Into communion wafers glowing
I'd blow sugar roses on
And call it dawn

The Day After

Dear Annie, I was staggered chasing,
Wasting this bright miracle
That blazed me freed on Grace's grass
At last two feet outside of Auschwitz.
Ninety pounds of new born human
Crawling after, you were crying.
I screamed Annie! Annie! Whispers.
Smiled then watched you turn and vanish
In the crowd of Tommy troopers cheering
I left hell to watch you kill me?
No Gestapo shock could break me
Living once more just to kiss you

Seeing you with strength for running
Hallelujah! Cringed then cowered
Felt my final spark devoured
On this messianic day
Oh Annie say you love me! Say it!
What did these grey demons make you?
Brick me up in Xyclon showers
Shunning April air without you
1942, the last I thought of time,
No time just waiting, praying
Raking bones on Sunder Squad
To scrape some news of you surviving

Maid to Monowitz Chief Steward
Smartly smitten by your beauty,
Always called your smile a blessing,
Seventeen and blonde and sassy
How you filled a sweater,
Classy, with a sure and calling swagger,
Flash backs dagger through my soul
To know you've taken hope away
Not one more heart beat lest a day
Can I abide this tortured cold?

Before I die my Annie write me
All I need to know is; why?

My Sweetest Joshie; Please forget me
That girl died and left this ruin
I've become a worn toilet
Torn and hard with hate and numb
I don't remember being human
I was their cow to ride and dump in
I was the bag they practiced punching
I was broken, busted, blackened;
Felt them vomit up inside me
Never mattered if they knew me
Threw me, fucked me where I landed,
Fucked me like my mama whipped me
A word, a stroke, a word, a cut;
I spit redemption with my teeth
Across the graves of love and trust

But I learned to love the comfort
Of the morphine and the gin.
Dusted from that dark infirmary
Servant to oblivion;

When she left me dry and hollow
What was soft turned cracked and harsh
I wasn't strong enough to end it
And I'm afraid I learned to march
For saving beatings. Learned to
Make them whine like Banshees
Some sick power grew each minute
I stayed breathing, don't know why
I lived in seething putrid rage and loathing,
Mostly for myself. And every grunt and thrust
Of meat and sweat I changed to bayonets
To gut them and remove my heart
In pieces sinking lower yet
Three years of looking up to Satan
Laughing at his shrinking whore
Prayed for steps down to the "showers"

Just to see you there once more
Josh you're all I ever loved
When I still lived and I could care.
But I'm no more, I'm worthless, nothing

Make this life that you've been given
I am waiting to be driven
Back to the patient arms of hell.

Maybe when you've made a family
And the wars for you have ended
You might find that girl you loved
With God in the Shoel

Dearest Annie only Lover
There is nothing real without you
I am stronger every minute
And I know "That" life has ended
But it's ended! Over! Past! It's History
This all brand new.
We stepped beyond the gates of death
We wept and worked for this beginning
Bathed in horror, filth and sin
And we survived to start again
Starting now with God's design
So take your time to let me love you

Honor her in her surrender
Let us burn and bury ashes
And bring love out of the cinders
Let the dead be dead in Auschwitz
They will still be dead without us

Midway

The side the big guy sits
Slips my mind each time
On the Octopus and Tilt a Whirl,
It's sacred Girl
To feel you crush on me
Hurling one care then another
Freed to houses of the holy
Prayers like rain leaves shaking hair
Drip sparkles fizzling in candied air

I would fill you with midway fair
Forcefully forgetting as we bet
On sticky tastes
And waste a million quarters
Showing you I suck at the arcade

If I can't be your hero
I would be your gallant clown
You can laugh and I claim victory
In gesture, wit and sound

But Darling bring you to my open mouth
To swallow up your pain
A sacrifice to happiness
And bleach it's bloody stain

Then again to win you teddy bears
And crash through coaster falls
To soak us dripping on a giggle
Dry then I could be your shawl
And share a twenty minutes kiss
While listing
All that love was ever
Severing the stress
And blessed the darkness

Do you think my plan is clever?

What Am I

Caesar cried;
Writhed in the sand slamming "Damn Its"
At a granite Alexander.
"26 his world was conquered!"
At 33 Caesar only owned what touched the sea.

Now look at me;
All I should be a fantasy,
A fleeting cheat of suicide
Piled double wide, crippled,
Suckling nipples ripe with lies.

What am I?
A sky plied with vodka bottle bricks
I fixed " jenga" style
A mile above an isle of my sanity
To climb to Jesus just to babble
Breaths of ash can revenants
Haunting candied apple causerie
In files of black bile gossiper wings
Taaka shots to gimcrack flings,
Wooed lusty skanks and pranks we busted

Beyond disgust
Again awake 'neath holey blankets,
Cold on cobblestone,
To hobble home lobbing gobs of baby aspirin
Washed back with ghosts of spirits I aspired to
That butts of cigarettes in beer cans truly
Kiss me like the morning, spent like youth
On routes to heaven by the fifth,
Silly twit.

What am I?
A faded whisper on the wind,
Wails of rumors blended in
With thin tin bells of rapture

Captured by a spell forgotten with a sigh;
Glorious as needles flying
From a withered pine crying through the winter
For a snow to tint it's brown and burning under white
One endless night.

I am a part of all I've past and some was good.
My portrait etched in scattered drift wood,
I'm wind borne chaff
Born to crash a bloodshot sunrise;
Pants at ankles mast
Saluting Mecca,
A heap of wrecked compact'd potential
Cowed in prayer;
Stoned, raw and bare,
Hands trembling scratching for a fix
I need
Revived by seeds
Contrived diseases mix
For freeing me of me.

I'd sell what bleeds in me,
Stained crumpled recipes forgotten
Bring little money at the pawn,
Repentant pleas through cans with strings,
Worn themes of schemes long dry of steam
I sing to God at Dawn.
I think he holds me when I cry
My lines get blurred in shady alibis.

What am I?
I am the moment I am in.
I've crashed the towers blitzed with sin
I gilded righteous.
I am reborn with every breath
An engine fired blast by blast,
An addict locked in loop;
I purge the man from me

With every step I stoop to,

An Unfit father
Of hope in burning spoons,
A tight Jacuzzi where I die not asking why
At 33 I hadn't even conquered me

What am I?
I'm still alive,
I am a vibe,
A work in progress.

The Fit

Is
A bottle of wine,
A hammer,
A beating bird on my earlobe
Listening to my mind talk
And humming back;

Ekphrasis wrecked
Between my jaw, my neck
That stains the brain
And changes breath
When time explodes
to glisten wet;

A line
On a blank page
That leaps, loops, plummets
To the base, I feel
It's real
Before it's ever traced,
Romance it
Dancing with the space;

A vision walling me in
Loud crowded rooms
Where far deep looks
Into racing brooks
Of conscious day dreams,
Unconscious shavings,
Frantic calling to the light
Escapes on passion
Exposed and minted
By the sun

Its masturbation,
Sex with ideas

Birthing blind
Sublimely tumbling
Locked to all and holding none

So never clever;
Bled in bed,
Compelled to sedentary travel,
The raw unraveling of gift handled clay
Before the play creating earthquakes
Or gusting winds blast trembling leaves
Broke to flagrant passes of the breeze
Tossed for gilding by the moon

Exhausted, snuggled in a swoon
And soon a cigar scents a laugh
For cutting, casts and craft
Not passion steered
Like God was not here

Dusk

Stumbling through a violet end day
Heavy, chilled and slightly bent
Past a beer born lover's tiff
I crumbled in a quiet heap

On a tombstone; sat by shade tree
Pounded fist with spit and vent
When to a note my senses went
Tied fast as reason met the reaper

In siren's hands my will decayed
A sorrow laden fiddle layed
A lazy, silken song a'sway
Sailing on a scent contented.

Wispy lovers, laced and fancy,
Rocking feet there
Locked in space
Filled to spilling; every kiss
A heartbeat doubled; another missed
A salty tear with dreams of sweet
Slid off her lips to wash his feet
And clung there like a mother stays
For year long minutes babies play
As seconds mint the past to lists

They grasped their moment
Doomed to mist;
Danced in an ether,
Oak cathedral
Blessed the grave I sat on feebly
Gazing from the fiddle's spell
I witnessed love the Ages held
With steps apart from year's advance
They fed the place with what they made
And days and eras danced from care,

I tasted what I'd never share.
I rose; I turned and changed
And there
I weighed extents of bliss that beat
Throughout my life's entranced charade.
I prayed to get a chance to seed
A love like one that fed the trees.

My caveat on "what you seek'
Like Smeagal's precious ring replayed,
Addicted slave half crazed with need,
My gift too loud for close appeal,
This phantom's grant commands I give
This gift to you so they may live
Then stumble back to watch the dance
Never feeling my own chance.

Then

Hallowed, happy, hollow times
Paper eggshell smoothly lined
Around a burning bullet's lie

For what had meaning
Wasn't matter anymore;
Rusted drapes of adoration from afar,
Parried grins
From Leonardo's quill,
Emmett Kelly thin
Your Mylar will,
Beguiling,
Tried; a strong and distant star

Still.
So much done was done too close
So much left was left too raw

And Then
Again tracing in the blue
Photos of the real you
Coloring the teeth in black

Always silly that way;
That day, you were dry then.

And I looked there
And wished you shared a peace with me
You, Like an angel with amnesia
Blew a kiss and peddled free
And lit the neon blurry streets

Ablaze again
But you wore shades then

Funeral For a Fat Ass

Going through that night the last time
Finely a finale playing
Credits syncing to a laugh track
Fat ass: himself
Red words on black

Epitaph was never more true
"Eating, eaten, no more breathing"
Ate his way right into hell
Cracker turned his blood to glue

In the lobby they were separate
Far from this, a modern leper
Slaven to a Twinkie poppy
Sloppy Bastard couldn't help it
Lucky, fuck he did us ok
One less whale to jack our Co Pays.

Rain came
Grey stained, weighty wind claimed
Left out poignant gleanings
Cleaning benches for a judgment day

Backspace! Silence!
You're a fly then.
Fast beeping busy flash it
"Hi I need the Priest
Forgive me
Only call him; please don't wake him
Father I can't live here longer.
Yes sir I can call tomorrow'

Dialing, ringing, ringing
Answer!
Fingering the steely Glock shine
"Hello St Jude Crisis Hotline"

Hi I need; I mean; I'm sorry
"Is this an emergency?"

Dial tone sound track
Fat tears gone splat
Downed like brokers on Black Monday
"Fuck me! Why not wait this night out"

"Fuck it! Do it Pussy don't pout
Always dragging lip and whimping
Eat another doughnut Blimpy
Doubting what you know is true
Everyone is best without you
Drain, you're but a bloated cancer
Your child's hopes are doomed to dancing
Helpless to your black hole mouth
Where your future's long been cancelled
Fat Ass ended. That's the answer"

I remember running, running
Running was like freedom to me
I could run my feet to bleeding
And then dance on tender blisters
All night long at Tipitina's
Life was X and Margaritas
Fiyo on the Bayou beating
Making love to Bacchus' sister
Going home to fresh purged ragings
Blurred through a distorted mirror

I have never seen myself
I guess;
Possessed by what was leering
Hatefully before me staging
orgies in my beaten body
Filthy cravings welding to me
Till my will dripped, sparkling fodder
Opening unclean revivals
My soul writhing
Legion driving

I remember healing something
Quieted for most my dealings
Now and then I busted frightful
Breathing in a peaceful feeling.
When I couldn't run no more
Swollen feet and broken right through
Guess I turned in pity's reeling
Peeling off the demon's door.

Sitting easy not to scare me
Slipped in hungry; said he missed me
Showed me comfort for the fear
All at once the mirror cleared
Fifteen years of treating me
To what had always been disease
Triggering my strength and will
Nor one more pants size shall I kill
Or Cookie snort or tart inhale
A rented room for a dying whale
Not endangered worth a care
Fare for punch lines, only fair
Won't even need St. Peter's scale
And better yes, yes they'll be fine
Bitter' Better. Do it.
Why"

Snack Bar Poster blinking wild
"Buy buttered popcorn extra greasy
Burnt in offering to 'Ole Beastey'

Eavesdropping in Ghostland

Peaceful I was, Quiet; right with death again
So sweetly pleased, so freed of feelings,
Dreamy flotsams cool as darkened dew
Serenely sprawled and yawing in the Zen.
Of all, in nothing was my proper place

Graced like glassy pond; lent tranquil waves
To shady trees and laying softly through the ethersphere
Far from Love and care and fear
Integrated into space
I was quiet then in no affair.

Oh but shattered sacred spirit's rest,
Serving Beauty in distress
Summoned full with rude intent
Killing what the calm had blessed
Another gentle throttling of sternums yanked
And rattling of bones and bells
As chickens bled in brick dust rings
And singing spells on beating things
With trances cranked by dancing
Sweat shined half bare breast

A face; Oh face like never seen
Now conjured in my consciousness
With Fate's full lips and eye that gleam
A trace of Fairy luminescence
Even angels Envy tests
When pressed to feel this art of God
In grifter's dress of gentle greetings
Gathered ancient manly greed
And eye walled chests and thighs o'er sod
On bearings trained for guns redressed
To oaken compass' throbbing read
Like laser's call to substance kneaded
Spun where lacy death receded

And purity her hand has played.

A volleyed tease of intimacy
Eating fruit of starved soul's cravings
So she planted corporal seeds.
When I awoke and stretched to faith
I reached to hold her soft with kiss
And swore to live for just her bliss
But knew what toll the outcome weighed

And fuck I marched without a prayer
But didn't hope just walked the fair
For thrills with price in naked waiting
Accepted bets were truly placed
And so it fell on raised, bent forearm
Without regret; I entered freely

Worth it? 'twas the only game
The tally once again the same
So Love, you ask, worth more than Peace?
Are flames worth more than all they harm?
A grande latte; I will fade
Oh ether bound where peace is made
Until she rattles blood and bones
When Love then obsoletes alone

Beside You

Beside you in bed
Beholding blood bred battlements
Soldered solid in silver suffering,
Transparent parapets
Buffering the cheaper tells
And bullshit sellers;
Keeping safely centered in your silent citadel.

I press my chest up on the glass;
Ask it to shatter by the shock
My beating heart in fits concedes,
My blessings counted in the inches
In between us, I'll glean my bliss
In parried *Parti pris* dismissed
Annealing healing,
Revealing my soul as clean
In scenes that time can't steal
Or stain or rust it into dust.
I'll trade my lust for trust
Beside you until truth
Looks warm and thrilling,
Fun and filling like a saving sun;
I'll lay and whisper dense devotions
In lavish fables, hopeful jests
And rest your fears
To clear the shadows
One by one.

I'll take my bliss
From this great distance inches spun.
I'll shun the hunger for your lips
Gripping tight the light
Against the wild winds of if
To hold on nothing I would miss
In the murky blue abyss
Condemned to reminisce

My blistering history of "shoulda dones".

No if tomorrow never comes
My only use for truth
Is won beside you.

Rainbow Runner

Two days passed the rainbow waned as fast as it came.
You called your game; and fled the scene
And your Face stained the world as plain,
Mundanely set, inadequate,
A skinny dream
Left wet to feign reality.
Well more or less

A feckless wreck but cut so cleanly
I confess
I'm rolling o'er an ocean's heavy emptiness
In sweet distress to feel for you;
Eyes on stand by, trying my searching soul
With sweeping reads; marking one place less,
In grey worlds blued by the truth of your absolute absence.

Silly how the scent of the environment went with you
Chasing rainbows, throwing ghosts and running from the real;
Feel a moth light sentiment you bolt then
On wailing winds wrestling loud around the silver sea
Breaking under me;

Taking all I knew of color schemes
For draping rainbows where I can't be
I pace the catacombs of my memory
To find a taste of you,
A trace of you.
I race for spacey notes
Ringing fat and clear,
With grace your lazy lightning brings
To sing through me with slight kissed waves;
To hear the decadent tsunami of your voice
That should wash this void away;

I miss you toying with the heart of those few days we knew.
I see your cat eyes laughing meanly

Like only cats can make it seem
So cool to be so cruel until
They need your fingernails
To reach an itching on their spine
But never whining
They sashay in kind appearance
Trailing tail like curling finger
Comely, calling, trolling in my heart's abundance,

I am the mark and you're the ringer
I'm laid open to your plunder,
Every cell a riot reaching for your skin again.
Sweet rip me raw then kiss me
While I beat a throbbing death in quiet
Under numbing, darkened endings
Under running rainbows lying
Crying prayers for lifeless worlds you leave
Chasing rainbows running where I can't be

Two days passed the day
The rain just lasts
The flames burn grey; the pale sun went
Two days looking for a life again
I'm glad you came but can't yet settle
And peddle searching far and fast
On rainbows running like the wind
To find that you are off to see
Another place that I can't be
A Dutchman flying endless seas
Your casualty of memory

My Place

On bloodshot horizons grinding
Blood hot grooves screwing
Hard against the glass clear black
I raise my breath.
I lie in quiet,
Denying the prima donna;
Defying the prejudice
Resigning me to die alone.
Everybody got a place

I lie in quiet,
Where the blues drag me around,
A flounder colored sloppy slipper
Slipping into coffee dark
Redemption
Doing mini-market weeks.

I fight
the windsong's whispering;
It's metal ink chilling
Glittered hieroglyphic butterfly
Painted characters, Kabuki style,
Demented gentle like.
Smelling cherry blossoms on Manchu wings
Selling spring in childish focus,
Chasing tastes like Crystal Hot Sauce
But everybody got a place.

I've waited minutes at a time
To live; forgive me.
I bubble back
Cruising Sazerac soupy sorrows,
Paying markers.
Cuz, I pawned my understanding.

Life, it bowls me till I stand again,

Re-paste the plans again,
Lift up my hands
Shouting Hosanna acapella
In swells of monastery peace;
Hollering Gospel
Where only light can hear.
You will know when I am near,
We'll celebrate us.

Everybody got a place
And it ain't never sweatin' the same spot
And when I got it
It comes with me,
It's brand new when I return.

Now to whom this may concern
You've earned to learn to let it go
I'll take your blues with me
And where I sew them
Light can swallow all the blossoms,
Fulgurant vulgar awesome stars
In flight
To make tomorrow on the magic
Dawn burnt off in honeyed dew.

From back the shrine for Brother Jude
I step through,
That pure first breath,
I bag the blues; hauled off for free.
Oh not for me but blessed and grateful I can still pay
To sit in now and then,
I play. I take the blues away.
Everybody got a place.

The Mojo

I held a raven's gaze
A hazy phrase of conscience pressed
In bending waves enveloped
Satin spun ruby fired reason
To lick against the lie of your indifference,
To swell incensed and bead release
The riffle heightening crests and seizes
Fanned; so elegantly gestured,

It's just you play to hollow ravings
And echo each dramatic pause
With fretful scratch
To keep the latch
On what is burning you

The raven smiles
My sly accomplice
Chanting meeting your soliloquy
Colloquial and slang interred
Billowed rhythms mix the words
Until you are replete with me
In dizzy fits of ecstasy

A fever beats and hunger pangs
A craving gravely stained
Ingrained to set on every meaning
Streaming past your steely heart
So shards impart sparks
To prime the fuel
The fire, breathe and burst
To bind desire to the flames
And feral urges claw and claim
What years of catechism tamed

And fly like succubus enraged
With wants of starving lioness

To mount me fierce as cyclones pounce
And grind possessed with streak and plunge
In choirs of Pentecostal tongues
Sumerian, harsh and condescending
Bending in inhuman flex
Consuming me by soul and ounce
Entombed by womb
I ripped from righteous

Now shadow's echo fights the Nothing
Wails in corners hiding dust
For the lust
Of a lisping Diva
The raven lights on phantom hand
"Best laid plans"
 The raven leaves

The Pit of Lingers

I reap the sting that the pendulum swing brings
And steep a tea cleared with teardrops
Then sweep the clingy strings into the pit of lingers;

I marshal shallow shadow circus car bazaars
Pulling trains on squeaks and crashes
Of thrashing beaks of preaching phoenixes
Circling freak wagons,
Flying tiger with scorpion stingers
On gator skin wings.

The pit sits bubbling on Nightmare Springs

Where shades of grey
Means you ain't seeing things
What is seeing you as prey,
A glib charade of being made
For Carrie's wedding
Lines dead again
The Overlook, snowed in again
And Jack the waiter's in the gin
With Reverend Steve, the twins,
Walking Man jammin the organ
Like Billy Corghan smashing stills
Of sassy demons sucking face
Wet bedding everyone you covet.

It's best forgetting what we're about to do
I would if I were you
This is a faith based education
Just believe me
And lean into me will ya?

Suraya

My heart did crawl with shock and awe appalled by bleeding fractal falls I sat with my Suraya on an easy vibrant day; to watch an acre cleared of Eden sheared and thatched by Claude Monet Between a liquid diamond brook and stony ivory covered wall

Of tangerine, mauve, rebel red; more greens and plums than words could call I asked Suraya "why would sling blade slay perfection for bouquet?" She giggled lightly saying "Faith of purpose;" sweeping me away where candle dragons swoop in currents playful, high in arctic wonder we communed in flashing pageant
setting quiet on the tundra
right to see a snowy fox
leap deep through snow for squeaky mousey lunch
I asked Suraya "why'd it plunge to ground so sure a rat was under?" She giggled lightly saying "faith of sense." We flew away again.

We caught a balcony at treetop where twilight mist and lonely lie two gothic lovers playing blood drunk cut too deeply then they died I asked Suraya why a wasteful gift seemed worthy of these lives she giggled lightly saying "Faith in love" then I broke down to cry and after sobbing I reached up to this my ether Asian guide but didn't need to speak she smiled and read the question in my eyes

"When we are grown into the light of love and living consciously
we are a part of greater purpose if we listen, feel and see
we trust our gut in all our senses with a ruthless certainty
we'll rip the roots from breathless brilliance if we're planting better seed we love to death if love requires though I usually disagree but walk in faith, in tune, in truth, in light and notice you are free and step with purpose
then just be."

Dwayne St.Romain, Louisiana storyteller, is evidence that creative drive transcends medium. A musician who took up poetry as a learning tool for songwriting, his songs have been published for A&M records acts and recorded by groups including the Neville Brothers and the Meters. His most recent poems published are "Walking Down Riverbend" in Women in the Company of Men from Edgar & Lenore Publishing House also "Flying Horses" and "Schizophrenic Born" featured in U magazine II and IV. His words are rich in visual and auditory experience best enjoyed when read aloud. Foremost he is a passionate and natural storyteller devoted to the idea the lyrically or poetically the story comes first. Look for his new works due out in 2012 and 2013 are in music the album "Ghosts of Harmony Church" by his band Baba Fatz; the novel A Groom's Tale.

Kimalisa Kaczinski

Breathing Room

He slid the balcony door open,
as she tapped the pack
of Pall Mall Gold's,
lighting her cigarette
by the flame
of a single match and watched
the feeding of snow,
silver sky, and the moon at full.
The pull of river was strong.

Flicking her spent cigarette
to the ground; grandfather helped
she return to bed. He sat
next to her in the lonesome chair,
drinking his coffee black,
his hand resting deep
in the thickness of her hair.

My grandmother's open eyes
returned to the balcony door,
they returned to the night
as she died with a breath of October.

This Used to Be a Love Poem

I don't have any pictures
of us anymore, I think I've given
them all to our son or perhaps some
met the fate of the paper shredder.
But the beach remembers our early days,
the shifting sand, the rolling water,
the pressure of your weight on top
of me. I wanted you inside of me
that night but you said there were better places
for us to be. I didn't agree but
I didn't get my way either. I think
this is a telling measure of our relationship,
I would've made love to you that night
with the moon and stars as our witness
but instead we ended up in a hotel room
and as soon as you were finished,
you fell asleep. I took a bath. Dreamed
of you being another man, a different
man. Would it have been any better
if I had gotten my way that night? You pushing
yourself inside of me with wet sand
as a cushion? I don't know. I do know that I would've
rolled on top of you and marked my
way into your body, I would've let
the pounding surf guide me, guide my body.
I would've kissed you with all my might.

This used to be a love poem.

Growing Crows

My sister grows crows in her backyard,
John says it's the finest thing he's ever seen:
crows with their dark eyes hopping along
her green picket fence. She grew a white crow
once, but he flew away.

The crows spend their time eating purple
grapes from climbing vines. They shed their feathers
and make the grass turn black. Sometimes the crows
take turns talking to one another, filling the air
with their caws.

My sister takes to her backyard at night, dances
amongst the crows, her pink satin nightgown glowing
with moonlight. She releases her breath, and the crows,
they capture it, the crows capture her breath and in turn
blossom into song. My sister says,

what music is this I hear.

Always a Train

for John

This is what it feels like
to be a poet: my friend John
says, there's always a train
going by when we talk…
I think of riding that
train and looking out over
softly rained upon valleys
and watching the mist rise over
one-church towns. I'll pick
up a leaf—they are only
veins after all—when I jump off,
fold it slightly and stick it
in my pocket. I'll forget about it.

I'll have to call a cab to get home
because really, who would I tell
my adventure to? Even John
who is also a poet, would he understand
my whimsy? Maybe. But for now I'll keep
the journey to myself, dream of whistles blowing
and cool air rushing my face. I'll think of
the green of the go light waving us through.
Come wash day I'll find the leaf
stuck in the dryer vent. It will crumble
in my hand from the heat, nearly
more than I can bear.

The Wish

Every few days I make another wish. The wish is always the same and will never come true, I know that. I wish for my dead child to be brought back to life. I might as well wish to understand the language of water. I'd give up my skin to have her back.

I have a Chagall print that hangs on my wall. It is called Self-Portrait in Green. I think the main figure is whispering to herself but I envision instead that she is whispering to my daughter. My daughter's name was Ruth. From the Hebrew, Ruth means, "friend of beauty".

In the Chagall print, the figure she is whispering to has dark eyes. They look sad. It must be how Ruth looks now. Or maybe I just imagine that. It's hard to look into the face of truth.

Every few days I make another wish. As if stars could cast shadows. As if dreams could have an end.

Sleep

We have lost tiny pieces of ourselves. Listen as our
teeth clink as we kiss. Our toes will dance
as if we were walking the high plains. My eyes
will hunt for yours and when morning comes, your
breath will unwind, find me waiting. Do our hearts
beat slower as we age or will we discover they beat
like a sparrow in flight? The stars will part ways
for us. Bring your body to mine. Sing to me and let
the music fall on us like oak leaves. It's not
enough to speak words of love, like any good poet
knows, show me, don't tell. Let the flowers grow
and you unfold yourself onto me and together

we will dream of the ocean, wait for the waves
to cover us, wait for the waves to make us warm.

Growth

We worked in the garden
today, my son and I, planting
yellow tulip bulbs, Jacob's Ladder,
a red rose bush. We miss Seattle grey,
the song of the ferry horn. The eastern
side of the state delivers us
days of heat, nights
of train whistle. We try to find
the rhythm, let it rock us to sleep.
The water works its way to our dreams
though, and we wake with fingers
stretching towards shells,
bits of polished glass. Sometimes we must
shake sand from our sheets.

In the garden today
I saw in my boy, the way he questions
self, questions life without
a father. I saw him look
at the dirt born under his nails,
accepting his knowledge of flowers.

Lass

For her, it was a good day
to die. She rode in the car,
my wild frontier dog, her head
hanging out the window, breathing
in the best of the last moments.
The vets did their job, pulling
the life from her, but she did
her job too, growling and sneering
until I patted her down.
Good dog.

I became resigned, glad that her tumor
would no longer swell. She let
go, her head resting on my thigh
as I dreamt of the grandest
meadow, free from traffic
and boundaries, good water
to drink and rabbits to chase.

Motherhood

The night my mother finally died I touched myself
with fingertips until I came. I wanted to feel
something. I thought about breaking the mirror
and cutting myself but that seemed too youthful.
Days gone past. It took ten years for her to die,
lung cancer. She would say those words as a whisper,
shame filling her. The windows are open today
and the breeze as it slides through is soft on my skin.
I saw her the other day, my mother that is,
except that her long black hair was cut short in a pixie
and dyed blond. I would've invited her for a drink
but I don't think enough time had passed. She should

visit me in small ways at first. Chime the clock, make my lamp
flicker on and off. Cast her hand against my shoulder.

A Sky Turned Blue

I want to dream that dream again, the one where our tongues meet in the middle and our lips grow soft, then sore. Kissing won't be enough we'll both agree. The sky will tremble and the blackbirds will chatter amongst themselves and soon you won't hear the sound blue makes. Poems will break apart, the nouns and verbs floating through air. I want to dream that dream again, the one where I am part of a whole. The one where night does not disappear and we glide over swollen stars. Whisper softly I will say and soon our bodies will be swept up in the fire.

I want to dream that dream again, the one where you sweep the hair off my brow and the evening primrose bloom in the moonlight. Our kisses will be heavy and our sorrows short. The wind will arrive, bringing tomorrow at our door.

American Girl

If on a night a long time ago, you find yourself with no place to sleep, get yourself to Winchell's. If you knock on the door long enough, loud enough, Mike and Byat will let you in; they will let you in to the world of donuts.

If you don't already know it, you will find out that donuts are deep fried, you will see the vat full of grease, smell the yeast and flour, and you will hear the deep throat of Tom Petty.

Later Byat will ask you to the drive in, and you will not remember the movie that played, or the taste of popcorn in your mouth,

but, what you speak of later (and you will speak of it) is the glow of a flashlight on your eyes during the kiss, hands on your body, the voice that tells you the movie has been over for a long time.

And this, this too is what you do not know: Byat will sit on a linoleum floor beside you, he will untie the long shoestring on his black boots, hand it to you and say, *here, take this, tie it around my arm tight*.

You will watch the needle go in, you'll see the spray, the blood, his eyes close, his head lean against the cabinet, you will see it all. Later, much later, you will dream with a big *what if* right on your lips.

If one night you have no place to go, no place to sleep, get yourself to Winchell's—watch as iron stairs are lowered from a ceiling, watch as Mike goes to his car, opens the trunk and takes a folded sleeping bag.

Watch as they walk the stairs before you, as you follow them, as the sky delivers itself to you.

As you rest your head on a night filled with roof access, you will be warmed by the way night swaddles you with a sleeping bag and a moon drawn just for you and if you had any doubts before, they are gone now.

The Pacific Ocean

It happens sometimes in families; the children grow up and realize if it weren't for blood, they'd have no connection. I wonder about the sister that didn't survive, was she the thread that bound us together? My father never got over the loss of her; he'd sit in his workroom and just stare at this polished tools. He never built anything else. I try to find her through my dreams, walk the old railroad tracks leading to the lake. Is she together with my mother now?

In my dreams mother appears in her old blue bathrobe. It is ratty, torn. I notice she is not wearing her slippers. What did she always say to us about that?—Put your slippers on before you catch your death of pneumonia—. I ask her—if you see my sister in the gloomy lake, will you tell her I am looking for her—? She disappears like the end of sky, all too sudden. I wake and my nose is filled with the scent of wild roses.

Once I pointed out deer to my next door neighbor. He nodded and walked inside his house. I never felt so fucking alone in all my life. My sister's name was Bethany. She loved the color pink and collected seahorses. She'd never see the ocean in her lifetime. The rest of us did, we drove to California the next summer. None of us could bring ourselves to swim. My mother loved her father, my grandmother loved me and I loved my sister. I taught her how to smoke, took her to parties. Mostly she sat in the corners of rooms, her face in a book. I waved to her now and then.

He Loves Me, He Loves Me Not

You lost
your virginity to me that night. Called out
Cheryl's name as you came. I understood
that, still holding you in my arms, and letting
you have another go at it. I taught you how
to be a man. The second time,
I came, and the only name on my lips
was yours. Oh Kevin, my Kevin. I wonder
if you are with her yet, your first love.
Was she as tender with you
as I was? Did she teach your tongue, your
fingers, to move over her body
slowly like a slow moving train?
The third time we came together, my first.
The next time that happened, I was married
and we felt the eruption like it was an electrical
shock. He said to me, did you feel that? And I did,
but what I was remembering was you. Is that wrong?

My life has been led through a series of Kevin's.

The first Kevin fell in love with me in the fourth
grade, he pulled my braids and sat next to me
on the bus. When he died, he was on his way
to pick me up. The second Kevin was you.
The third Kevin? We were two ships that passed
in the night, never quite connecting and now, I've
lost his phone number. The fourth Kevin, I broke
his heart and my life has never been the same,
I whisper his name through the open window at night sometimes.
But this poem is about you, Kevin the second.
I remember how pale your hands were, and the way
you shook when you entered my body the first time.
I would've held you all night but you had to check on her,
your Cheryl. She was as young as we were but yet I think
of her as being just a girl. A girl waiting to find
the shape of her own heart.

The Cool Side of the Bed

for Larry

and the cool side of the bed

I whisper you across time
        and place—do you hear me?
                the wind travels down—
my fingers stretch towards the thought
      of you, then come back empty
like a glass left to sit on the countertop for days or weeks
            remember me? I'm the girl who sat
on the hood of your car and smoked Marlboros
      in the rain
      the driving rain

I whisper you through the long nights
       through the open window
and touch myself

I wonder: where have my dreams gone?
       is yours the only face I will ever see?
     does it mean something to you that I can't breathe,
        that I can't sleep   without the thought of you?

the smell on your pillow lingers
how long has it been?
         only a lifetime

I whisper you a moonlit night
          and the blurry stars in my eyes
tell me
             I've done nothing wrong
except love you   love you
love the thought of you

Crushed

I slept with the boy with the yellow t-shirt. His hair combed back from his face, and this: he said he had a dream where we moved his bed outside underneath the weeping willow and made love with only the stars watching us.

I could have crushed him with my love.

We smoked Marlboros and drank Rolling Rock, the green glass reflecting expectation and desire. We could have made a bed of straw by the fire. We could have danced all night, the moon guiding our steps. Instead we spoke of love gone past and passed a joint.

Shine I said. He said I wish we had doughnuts, the kind that melts in your mouth. He was a man lit up. Our hands touched. His mouth was on my breast. We passed out with his head on my shoulder.

I dreamt of quiet things. We woke up and thrust our bodies against each others. We kissed out loud. The sun was unblemished, the fire was out. It was a long morning, and when we were done I knew it was time to go. Some things you can't improve upon.

Let us imagine this: I drive away and he runs after me, he runs after my car with the dirt and dust blowing in his face. I think he yells stop.

Orion's Belt

We were so young back then. Those were the days of disco and 3.2 beer, the Hustle and bell-bottomed pants. I never could dance but man, I loved the music. My boyfriend Chad and I were regulars at Orion's Belt, our favorite discotheque. Stars were painted on the ceiling and when the disco ball lit up, the stars, they sparkled.

One night, Donna Summer's song, "Love to Love You Baby" came on and Chad and I, we began to kiss. Oh how I loved him. There wasn't anything I wouldn't have done for him. Our kiss had heat behind it, a relentless tantalizing heat. I could feel the pressure building. We were sitting in a U shaped booth. I let go of Chad's lips and slid under the table. I unzipped his jeans, taking him in my mouth. "Love to Love You Baby" segued into KC and the Sunshine Band's "Keep it Comin' Love". No one knew what I was up to.

I took Chad's hand and placed it on my naked breast. I released him from my mouth and tugged on his other hand. Now he was under the table with me. I pushed down my jeans and took him inside. Our lips were fastened together. Our bodies moved as one to the beat. Maybe I couldn't dance but I sure could fuck. When I was about to come, I opened my eyes, looking around me and saw the lights from the disco ball sweeping the floor. Chad was staring at me and our eyes locked. It wouldn't be much longer before our faces were revealed for what they truly were.

Tess, as She Moves

I say it's good to remember your first fucking boyfriend. The boyfriend that only wanted to fuck all day long.

Once we climbed a fence to reach the overpass and on a starless southern California night, he fucked me on top of the Creeping Charlie.

Blossoms of headlights floated over us as we came.

We fucked in the bed he shared with his wife and he said, Tess, the only place I ever want to be is inside you.

When he'd say, you'd be smart to listen Tess, I would.

Other lessons he taught me:
You're responsible for birth control.
Listen long enough to the river and you'll be surprised when the rocks burst into song.
Don't leave me.
When we dance, just follow my lead.

One night we fucked underneath a table in a bar. Our bodies moved as in an earthquake.

I know that nights he wanted to go dancing, it was best if I drank a lot. I never could follow the moves in the two-step.

That night by the overpass, the birds flew over us. They must not have known we were there. I opened my mouth and tried to catch breath from their wings.

The Night I Met Richard Gere

I was at a movie theatre one night and I met Richard Gere. I saw him walking down the aisle shaking hands. When he got to me, I looked in his eyes and saw how tired he was. I held his hand tight and said to him, and how are you this evening? I think he appreciated that. I'm sure everyone else asked for photos or autographs but I thought that just this, holding his hand and seeking a connection was enough for me to remember. I mean after all, isn't he just a person, just a person like me?

He answered that he was fine, running a little tired but that he looked forward to these moments of greeting people. I think he looks for something in that. What I mean to say is that he also seeks those connections that are sometimes meaningless and second-nature in respect. His eyes. They held on to mine and I felt calm.

I remember once swinging in the park. I was by myself and really pumping my legs to gain speed. I wanted to fly. For the first time in my life I felt brave, willing to jump and waiting to see where I would land. I didn't do it though. I slowed down and lingered. The swing soon enough came to rest. I regret that now, but what is regret but perhaps a chance to do something over? I still haven't done it, fear is the great divider in some of us.

Isn't it funny, I don't know what movie played that night and I don't know where I was or if I was by myself. Richard Gere leaned over and whispered in my ear before he left. I forget what he said.

Husband Number Four

Look at the preacher man holding that gun. Perhaps he'll hide it behind a book about Matthew the Apostle, wings spread wide across the cover, or this: the preacher man's hand deep in his pocket—thumb caressing black steel.

And there has to be a moment devoted to the mother, her skirt that evening, how much of her ample thighs were concealed, her earrings, were they chosen to match the color of her shoes or the eye shadow so carefully applied?

One last look before she walks out the door, *perfect*, she says.

Preacher man smells her before he sees her, baby powder; *it keeps my thighs from chafing*. And those puckered full lips; oh she knows how to use those lips.

She wouldn't even begin to notice him, of that he is certain.

He sets Matthew down, *careful, don't crease the pages,* and slides the gun out of his pocket. It is warm from his contact and feels good in his hand.

He thinks that perhaps in this moment in his will take shape. He's been dreaming about this for so long, knowing where he will take his shot, right eye closed, hands steady.

Preacher man takes sight of her bottom—draws the trigger.

The mother manages three steps before she falls to her knees.

Marvelous is his thought, the gun hot in his hand, *they really do smoke.* It was never his intent to kill her.

He wanted only this: the mother brought to her knees.

She remembers her children in Florida, how it seemed those Atlantic waves might crush their small bodies. They ran, wanting her to join them, experience the feeling of walking underwater.

Lake Powell

I get so lost in my own head
at times. I go outside to smoke
in between lines of poetry. Lately
I've been noticing butterflies.
A lot of butterflies. So I looked them up
to see what they symbolize. Thinking maybe
I need to be paying attention. Butterflies
mean transformation. Is it me that's looking
for a change or is it in regards to my poetry?
I don't know but I do know
that they are simply beautiful.

I've been trying to write a poem
about my marriage. We met on a Saturday
and he proposed on the following Wednesday.
We were married two months after that.
I wish I had worn the red shoes I coveted instead
of the white. Then I would've had
something that was just about me that day.
But, I wanted to please, and red shoes weren't
'appropriate'. I laughed when I placed the ring
on his finger. We should pay attention to signs.

I stayed married for twenty years. And I'd go back
and do it all over again for the pleasure of having
my son. He needed both of us to create him. On the night
he was conceived we were on a houseboat on Lake Powell.
We had the upper deck to ourselves. The water had been
rocky that day. Everyone else got sick, but not Bob and I.
That night, the water
was calm and we laid under the stars on a sleeping bag.
As we were making love, I felt the change. Something different.
A transformation you might say.

I won't get married again, not worth the risk
of losing so much of myself. I was devoted to him

and he was devoted to the bottle. I spoke to him just the other day.
He answered the phone and when he heard it was me,
he said, hey girl, how's it going? He was a kinder
version of himself. We talked about the years. I didn't bring up
Lake Powell. The water that day. How it was just he and I
facing the waves head-on.

Finding Poetry After The Mountains Have Gone Away

I miss you; I miss you like I'd miss my own breath. I wake from a dream where the mountains have gone away and all I can see is the flatlands of the prairie. I remember once asking you, don't you have any scars? And you replied, they're all on the inside. You hated your parents. Wondered why they'd taken you from your homeland. When you shot up on the floor of the kitchen, I removed the needle. I watched you fade away. Heroin for the hero of the story. I wish I could have been your heroine. I don't know where you are buried, isn't that incredibly sad? The last time I saw you, you were watching Cheers on television. Your back was turned away from me. We had kissed earlier that day, long, slow kisses that reminded me of nothing. Sweet Jane you called me. Do you remember holding my hand when it meant everything? We went fishing once at the lake with no name. We threw all the fish back in. I couldn't believe how silky they were to the touch. I'd go back to that lake if I could, and I'd gather all the white stones, settle in on my back and watch the sky turn faint.

Snow

It was the first snowfall of the year and as I sat in the windowsill watching fat flakes fall to the ground, I remembered the time he told me that he loved me. I was in my bedroom when I heard the slightest ping; he was throwing stones at my window and I heard him yell, I love you. How many times does that happen in your life? He was my first. We were both virgins. When we finally made love, he said, baby, am I hurting you? And I answered no. He gave me a heart necklace made of gold. I wore it for years, losing it one day while I ran the track of our high school. I looked for it forever it seems. It was the last thing I had that he had given me. All I have left are the memories: playing putt-putt golf, kissing in the rain, playing truth or dare, the night we conceived. I lost the baby five months into the pregnancy. We decided to name her Jesse. She's buried in a cemetery under the loveliest of oak trees. I haven't visited her in years now. He's buried in Seattle. The pain of losing Jesse was just too much for him. He died of a heroin overdose. I hope in those last few moments he stretched his arms out wide to catch her.

Let Us Go Then You and I

~for Dwayne

Breathe me a lullaby with your eyes
Here, winter is a river blue
Let me go and hear me sigh

Together we will watch the sun rise
Trace our finger over the dew
Breathe me a lullaby with your eyes

Wait for the sky to baptize
Us clean through and through
Let me go and hear me sigh

Let us go then you and I
To the place where we came to
Breathe me a lullaby with your eyes

Whisper to me as the wren flies
And I'll take time to say thank you
Let me go and hear me sigh

Open our arms to the welcoming skies
Feel the sense of déjà vu
Breathe me a lullaby with your eyes
Let me go and hear me sigh

With nods to Larry, John and T.S. Eliot

Kimalisa Kaczinski lives near New Orleans, Louisiana with her partner, the poet and songwriter, Dwayne St. Romain. She finds most of her inspiration comes from that which she finds outside, primarily with birds, water and flowers. Her work has appeared in many fine journals, including The Massachusetts Review, Floating Bridge Review and Eclipse.

James Crafford

The Nebulous Labyrinth

Crawling like a blind python out of the darkest regions of hell.
I have no appetite except the hunger to get out of here.
I know my stench is wicked and my face frightening.
I haven't had a morning erection in a month.
My dreams are filled with drowning in a cesspool of despair.
The noises I make in my sleep would keep a dead man awake.
I worm forward like a dirty eel through the nebulous labyrinth.
Reeking of loneliness, suffering from head to tail.
How did I lose my way and fall so deep into this pit?
I think it had something to do with love and the futility it births.
I think it had something to do with that brick wall I tried to
negotiate with.
I took a peek at bloody Jesus all whipped. I know how he feels.
I read some crumbled pages of Upanishads and Dhammapada
but the spiritual comfort zone I expected only burnt.
I know I am still alive. I can hear the motorcycles roaring in the
distance.
Night is permanent and day is gray.
I lay on my left side, my right side, my back and breathe.
I am warm enough. Thank God.
Maybe if I crawl a little further into the maze I will find my way.
And maybe I will have to turn around and begin again.

The Nebulous Labyrinth pt 2

The roaring motorcycles are symbolic of my escape.
Late into the somber evening I can hear them and
Just knowing they are there gives me relief and hope--like an
injection.
Fuel injection.
I can picture myself riding in a B Hollywood movie with you
on the back clutching to me, too young for me, too beautiful for
the phantom
I have become (while my wounded face heals).
Dreams are suffocating like too many blankets.
Like too many slippery damp pillows
Covered with my sweat and my struggle.

I am teaching myself how to eat with utensils
and teaching myself to talk without howling.
I take cautious baby steps toward the bathroom
Where I lose my balance and fall into the darkness
As a used tissue falls into the waste paper basket.

One day all of this will be as forgotten as ancient tales.
It will bake in a merciless sun in a merciless dessert
and will be obliterated by the elements.
I will be free and riding without a helmet.
Fearless like an outlaw wanted in all fifty states

Dirge On a Stormy Afternoon

washed away and drowned in your beautiful kind of sadness
washed away yet nourished simultaneously
the stern delicacy of your moves
the pliant statuesque mask you wore
sentimentality cracked
nostalgia shattered in a neon desert
those whom knew us wept
those that did not know us laughed vulgarly
the trap we had sprung failed like dull soup
our escape into neutrality faded as a shadow
the telephone became a diseased gadget
the typewriter no longer held ribbon of two colors
that job we had together at the carnival!
(those freaks we worked with!)
that cliff we walked to the edge of
(that ocean we refused to swim in)
i felt your sadness like blankets
and those blankets caressed my heart

A Shy God Hiding

my god is timid/he is hiding under a bridge/like a troll/he gives out his address to

no one/he allows no visitors/he is not hospitable when guests arrive/he is not

even a he/he is not a she either/he is an it/my god is shy/he hides/he sighs

silently/he has earplugs in his ears when i pray/i rarely pray/but when i do/my

god is too embarrassed to hear/he hides under a bridge like a troll/my god does

not like to be obvious/he is subtle/subtle like thunder and subtle like acid

rain/when i cry out for him/he runs in the other direction/he doesn't want to deal

with me/he's heard it all before/all my troubles/all my doubts/all my faith in him/he

can be stingy and difficult/not the god of abundance or the god of lilies of the

field/my god is a timid scared god/a god afraid of people/afraid of war disease

and death/he created it/but he will not embrace his creation/he hides under a

bridge like a troll

Me and Circe Make a Go of It

I admit I was lured by her voice
and knew from the get go
that she lived in a cave.
One way in and no way out.
It wasn't that she sang so good
that captured me. It was that
she sang at all.
With her face away from me
at the rainy windshield.
The splash of rain drops mixed
with her semi-harmony
singing along with the CD player
in the car.
I said, "Where do you live?"
And she answered, "In a cave down the road."
When we got there, I saw that
it was a hole in a rock shaped like a mouth.
I knew it would devour me but
I did not expect to be chewed.
I stumbled and fell as soon as she released me.
I found my way to a footpath below and
limped forward with the help
of a walking stick made from my own blood.
Now when I think of her voice
it brings a little laugh along with it.
A giggle from hell.

(after reading The Islands by H.D.)

The Microscopic Report

I am just a speck in an infinite womb.
But I smell and taste and sometimes see
And often hear a low rumbling in the distance.
 I am only a tiny bud on an infinite tree.
But I have made love to you for hours
And I have written you poetry from my soul.
 I am only a miniscule amoeba floating
In a monstrous ocean, but I have
Memories that sting me into Awareness
Like a benign electric chair.
 I am small. I am diminished. I am ground
Beef in a dog's food bowl
But I feel the now spring breeze while reading
In an old chair outdoors. A breeze that
Penetrates armor.
 And my size in perspective vanishes.

The Dagger of Neglect

The dagger of neglect lies silently under the pillow.
There is a blanket, dirty with the dust of lies
That wraps its filthy weight around our doubts.

Most of the time, the blinds are closed,
The stairway is empty, the closet doors
Remain unlocked.

Sometimes the dawn is seen and sometimes
It is not.

Night, with its secrets, steals into memory
Like a virus, dragging an invisible body bag.

I am going to stab you and you are not
Even going to feel it.

Chrysalis

I am a fetus within my own womb.
I am dangling, waiting, nurturing
My soul within a chrysalis
Of my own sacred engineering.

I have a million mile journey
Ahead of me.
I own no maps, no radar.
It is all instinct that will get me there.

I will form friendships and battle enemies.
I will surrender. I will be victorious.
I will breathlessly stall in stalemate.

This chrysalis that protects me
Will tear open.
It will release me.
And I will fly, soar, glide and swoon
Into the unknown future.

Like a squirrel I am storing up
For the winter of my discontent.
Like a turtle I am hiding in my own shell.
Like a butterfly my fragility is my strength.

The Impermanence of Mothers

The buildings, the streets, the trees, the stone walls
all seem so solid and real
yet you are gone

Your reptilian skin has vanished
The frozen frown on your face evaporated

I miss you more this time than I care to explain

I am standing near your grave in Notre Dame
with the January breeze toying with my emotions
and ridiculing my mortality

I picture you claustrophobic in your coffin
banging on the lid

Within the Unseason

I am resting comfortably in nothingness
that pillow of oblivion

No snow no rain no wind
that unseason of the void

Lightning no more and thunder obliterated
that sightless soundless lull of sleep

Within the unseason
I dream of my mother

She throws a roll of paper towels at me
as a means of drying my eyes

When I awake from dawn infested reveries
the celestial cellos are playing again

The melody is unfamiliar
but the refrain is as a childhood rhyme

Tonight I will rest again
within the unseason of a mortal soul

James Crafford is an award winning playwright and screenwriter. He won the Jean Dalrymple Best Playwright Award 2004/2005 and his indie film CHEPACHET (based on his play) won two Best Drama Awards at The Indie Gathering in Cleveland and The New York International Independent Film Festival. Jim is a professional photographer who specializes in natural light headshots, glamour and fine art (www.jamescraffordphotoraphy.com) . He is currently at work on a personal theatrical memoir about the legendary teacher Stella Adler and his numerous adventures Off Off Broadway. Jim lives upstate NY with his wife, Linda, and rottie, Tyson.

Caili Wilk

The invisible light

I never understood how
love and hate spill so carelessly
without seemingly a thought
to their telescopic quintessence.
They are inseparable. Sky & stars—
an unending canvas for astonishing
brilliance all the more stunning
in the darkest night, healing even
our destructive history inconsequential.
We deserve no more, no less than this.

The light has changed

Spring blooms earlier here than it does in Europe.

I still cannot forgive myself. Panic comes from nothing
and from everything. The beat of my heart is faster than
it ought, my thoughts today are rabid: how quick the tumble

how small the trigger. There are so many things I need
to take care of—freshly cut grass, California poppies.

There are skies deeper than all the sadness I ever
felt, where clouds are neither pink from the sunset
nor grey from a gentle thunder. They hang low, close
enough to jump right through, lighter than a wing of bird.

A heart is not infinite & God does not punish
or give. There are so many things I need to take
care of.

the feast

i'm not eating lunch today
have decided
to write a poem

instead
of hard cheese, soft bread
and mayo

besides
you drove the car
out of gas

and
the red apple
i brought is enough

after eating the morning news
& framing
the email from God

Asecular Spirituality

If we must talk of religion, then speak
in peace not tongues; of inner gratitude
not worldly possessions. A woman told
me recently God gave her a grand house
then confided she'd left all her friends
behind & now had 3 extra bathrooms to
clean. I can't imagine whose God would
leave her lonely cleaning all day, but she
beamed & praised him for the extra sq
footage, as those with true faith publicly do.

There are too many friends of mine who
are trying to die. So disturbed by the world
& how awkwardly they belong to none or an
infinite number of responsibilities. I try
to stop imagining how I will hear of their
successful attempts, or how they will hear
of my own crooked walk to the gates.

When is it appropriate to dwell on these
things? Is it when the sound of nothing gets
a little too loud & loved ones are too far to touch?

How comforting it must be to think we are never alone.

Honesty

Reading the book first, or after,
almost always spoils the film.
The fecundity of our own bizarre
invention, theoretical imagination;
the methodical black print, paragraphs,
periods, a typo here and there; even
a conveniently placed character
in the next chapter convincing us to live
another season of regret, late in the
afternoon, unseen on the front stoop.

We survive, immeasurably, on our own
continuous lies, surpassing even themselves
so rapidly, they trip is during the execution.

As I fall unnoticed, I write some more.

The Mistake

We find no
comfort
in
truth; consequence
is what
we prepare
for.

A single
moment
cut
a thousand ways
yet
we see no
difference
& fall prey
too often
to
misguided
wisdom

Echos
scar
like glaciers
the earth.
Today we brave
the wind
but it lives
on
when we die.

Ice

You may understand I do
in fact
love you
not just adore you
or worship you more
than you think you deserve

I love you for no reason
& there should be no reason

True
you are
nothing special
nothing really can be
yet this
unforgettable
accident
pervades me in
cascades of clarity

I fear you deeply
as I love you
I don't want to fear you
yet I wonder
if love
will turn you away
as we wrestle
untrusting the other

Your doubt
in you
in me
in us
it does no good

believe me

if the trees did not bend today
or the afternoon
was not
beautiful grey
I do not love you

I would rather die
than lose my memory
of this time

I would rather lose
my memory

than you

Regret

I
sometimes i wish to
move this heaviness
taste once
with my eyes closed
only
as our
death
breaks
the future functions
into
resemblance
of breathing
look   left   right
walk toward
tumble into
the killing so slow

II

We leave it till next week to
talk, you suggest, over lunch,
figure out what is going on
between us: is it just a little
crush best left untouched?

I feel out every scenario and
still come back to the idyllic
romantic version that we should
just allow ourselves to fall in love
for the day, or week or year.

III

all day
cleaned house
drank coffee
didn't stop
why me?
judge & jury
of these
pitiable actions
just mistakes
that are
not all mine
sorry is
so useless
sour reeling of
vomit & pain
cleaning
organizing
throw it
all away

IV

your twilight traced face
your eyes I cannot turn

we might as well
perjure expertly
be skilled in something
other than regret

my own
faded ache believes it
    a tiny emptiness
    everything is stable
    everything resumes

after the party, in a grassy lot

you almost
do not exist
soon no trace
no proof any
thing about
you ever
happened

we almost kissed
almost fell apart
& across the hood
across a time where
our eyes couldn't
see our minds

the moon
    hung in half a starry sky

cars kept
    driving dimly by

Rites

A man is barking, leaving Starbucks. He makes more sense today than a nebulous sky. I am just too tired to feel the world sigh, and defend the unusuals from the normals. Is this detachment what ordinary people must endure each day? Everywhere, you are there and there you are not. I pray for safe passage and calm. It seems we all will travel the same journey, till then, debate the destination. The unmarking is not possible or wanted. I don't even mind the coffee spilling down my shirt.

Rainbows

Eating a waffle, Bourne exclaims *it tastes like Sally!*
Yesterday he slurped on cotton candy blue yogurt,
said it was the same as his favorite brown truck.
I wondered if he had his senses mixed up
like me, if sounds came when there
should only be touch, if music has a color
and happiness looks like a floating orb.
I didn't want to worry him with questions
so I asked him for a taste of Sally instead.
He shared his waffle with me, dripping
Beethoven's Moonlight Sonata.
We giggled as I wiped away telltale
flecks of rainbow from his mouth,
then left to collect Gabby.

Phenomena

Sometimes experience comes
in an opaque box
or a dewdrop frozen
in stillness.
I can reach out and peel away
infinite fears & delights,
as I would petals,
freeing them to seed
till they are soundless air
enfolding me.

My thoughts are yellow,
spheres the size of ugly fruit.
Occasionally I split them
open, drink the flood of
neon, leave a useless mass
of deflated skin which slowly
blows away into the unmade sky.

California

The light here is violent. Each tarnished pasture lit too bright to hide among its herd. Santa Ana pilfers every third thought: people toast the future in all its eventual corrosion.

In the shade, walnuts scatter. The fruit falls early this season, like the remnants of youth often do with each generation. Somehow, this was never conjured, even within my especially idyllic version of events. Always, the sky was warm; the sun, mute.

No glare, no Hollywood sign.

Driving the curved canyons should only be done listening to Amadeus in a white soft top, (as a passenger), then brunch. Malibu. The rich artist's beach pad. Sometimes I remember my first visit as it really was: Chess before it rained; sour cream, the limo ride & goodbyes. I had never seen fruit so big before.

Summer

The grass is brown; a collapsed vein of lung.
We fall, stunned when the bottom greets us
before we embrace our decision.

No method, nor variance;
sweating, half drowned
amid this heartless beating of pace.

Some caged animal
we are, lying & sunning, somewhere asleep,
unhinged, useless of protect.
Yet even as my knees buckle under the weight
of your remoteness, I want to fold your despair
into next year's reminisce, crumple it.

This doesn't feel like summer should feel.

The sky
so
unmessy & blue.

The sun
so
bloodless a coup.

Historical Materialism

The tension is unimpressive,
dull; could be forgotten in the sand.
An antique blade sold at the store
for less than the American buffalo.
No wonder the excuses
ring hollow, the highlights fail—
persuade only if you didn't pay close attention.

Don't tell, but I think
this is the big one;
the fucker of all fuckers
but without the guns
& flashing lights;
the war of words; of virtue
of reason, save the mediocre poli-tactics.

Afterwards, you better
not say who you voted
or why, demand the
bourgeois to reply "as long as
you did", leaving all chance of
argument tightly would in their smile.
De Tocqueville, in his grave,
reluctantly coming to terms,
is still right. The enemies
of the state have individual rights,
express the opinions against the majority will,
can be thrown in jail because of it.

I can't vote: I'm not a citizen.
Instead, I'm sitting observably bored
you might think when in fact just desperately
tired & a little unhappy, seeking
control over my life, paying too

much attention to believe it's possible
to be with or against
the majority till they actually win.

As a child my mother would cram
the cooler box full, cram us
to a park, a bench, an island in Paris
where we would play all day,
homing in only to eat, as she sunbathed topless
packed up once the cooler contained only refuse.

I never saw her prepare the food
or recall her even eating.
She was a single parent
working on minimizing her tan lines,
escaping into another cheap paperback
smoking another pack
not thinking about
feeding the electric meter,
or the Native American Bison.

Impact

The colonel is dead, the unemployed said.

But I have no time to read the news, or reflect on what this means for the world, who is lined up to dictate the future 40 years.

I don't care about old men with dandruff wearing ill fitting hats. So what if they have angry faces and unjustified places. I need to get to work on time without stopping for coffee or a quite place to contemplate my rethink.

I need to lie to another person in my life, not sit around measuring its unique de-meaning. The news of the day belongs to those who can: can still feel the pang of sadness at the sight of what just isn't natural.

But really who cares? This isn't some highly hated reality TV show.

Only the unemployed these days have time to watch and swell from their steady unledge.

Yes, you will be there a long time, better get used to it.

And while you're at it, stand up for my rights while I collect too small a pay check. Occupy Wall Street phooey baloney.

We all want the bigger pocketbook.

And I want that beach house with 2 master baths: a lap pool, red convertible and the sky is the limit. I don't want time for a quite place to think. I don't want to cry for anyone, anywhere, anymore.

The mood is rad, blinking sad.

    Who needs to know which colonel is dead?

They say it each fall, next to the half page diamonds will bring tears to her eyes, so buy it at 30 % off ads.

Reminiscent

I understand but am trying hard not to. I like to pretend I'm a little less worldly, that I've never seen the eye of the storm, no-one sucked out my blood in this lifetime. This feeling is pointless & predictive: a shameless mirror of the trust I have for you. Have I told you how it frightens me that I don't remember why we are here; when I'm happy and my brain denies me memories, the craziness becomes even more real than what is right in front of me? I still fear the pain; avoid its encounter but I'm not as cold as I appear.

This does matter, and I don't know how it will end.
Funny how things never end before the end.

Larry Kuechlin

Departure From Shalford Rail Station

for Chris Madoch

I used to know the way.

I used to know the way beyond
the tired rousing of leafless miles that wind
the North Down

around a tortured Oak
that died on King's Road the day it was born:
I used to know each deaf step past
the rattled accusations of
      winter's ebony reach:
a forced contrition of life stolen
         promise by fall.

I've come back to the Shalford Rail Station
      to hold the shadow's place

      and wait for you

while beggars rummage a darkened sun
for a solitary remain of grey.

      On the platform, I wait as
students huddle around a glow in open hands:
rumpled packs of Clove cigarettes;
         the closing snap of a Zippo;
they seep back into dark pockets filled with
a Bell's half and small volumes of poetry;
the freedom of George Orwell and Ayn Rand:
      incendiary ideas of a Welsh Poet;
words of the Sea, barely recognisable in the wear.

I watch them all:
the jumpers, blazoned in pub chic

    and the dog-eared signs of youth;
    they disappear behind departing doors;

but you are not there.

Alone, I falter at the platform;
    turn up cold's collar against my mind
    and wear darkness like a mac.

At the end of the station
a Girl sits at her laptop;
    beautiful in a way she will never believe.
On her way to London;
    offices and upward mobility
that belie the secrets kept in the cast of her eyes:
I hold them long enough to know
    there is no sadness like hers.

I reach into my overcoat
and fumble through Family Court notices
    and debtors demands
until I find the reason I am here:
    the one last door you slammed shut by Post;
an envelope with nothing more than
a departure stub from the Shalford Rail Station.

I stare beyond causation and
so very badly,
    I want to fill every cut with

    the quiet light of a bedroom door
    the weight that settles under a smile
    the drowning sigh pressed against your forehead

and all the gentle imperfections of love
from a man who has never found its end:

a man who is never off his knees
even when he has to be strong;
    a real father

                    who gathers you
in moments and mending
            that burn so brightly
                Heaven itself burns down around him:

I want to fill your closed fists
            finally

            with a heart that never fails:
to steal the loss away from your smile
and everything that calls me down the icy press

            of falling under a face full of rain
            of concrete against my knees
            of fire against my palms:

the solitary madness
            accounting loss
while afternoon shuffles always away
and my body speaks a truth that goes unseen;
            something imminent and broken.

I look out of windows filled with the lash of
dead hands deep in a raven's wing.

Harrow Wey chokes down
            the rustle of summer's dying breath.

    Empty cups tip against the tatters of a draining sky.

I watch the Girl, now waiting on the platform;
        her pea coat sways into a passing train
and I think of all that is missing.

Sainsbury wrappers and Walkers bags
rush away behind its departure
            into the reckoning
of endless days I come back here
                        waiting for you:

waiting to hold your hand
        softer than the burden of light into my chest;
to feel the weight of your youth on top of my feet
and dance you into
        the white moments of your forever;
to swing you off your feet
                like I used to do
and circle a sky beyond the aged grief
where sorrow drowns into the wishing:

    and to hold you;

just hold you,
        torrent to scar
with arms that can be full only in your smile;
to lower my dreams onto your head
and smell the desperate light of your hair,

deeper than henna and stars;

deeper than prayer and assent;

        but I am alone,

adrift in a blur of stubs and
the sound of eternal doors, dark in their throes.

        The wind fills an open window with glass.

A white bird rises into
        an evening bleeding crow and

                always rain,

        but my body will not rise with it:

I used to know the way.

Acrylic on Canvas

Contained in Waterford crystal,

mangos and pears sliced open;
left to bear the weight of
the beautiful blade that bid them asunder.

        Croissants and blackberry jam;

a forward stroke of sunlight
a staccato return of amethyst and

                              soft laughter;

silver flatware bearing fresh butter
left abandoned, next to a small volume on the table

    Keats, Thomas,   Neruda
        (the sigh is all the same)

dog-eared and worn open
by a missing hand;

dark coffee, dark sugar
and a damp towel draped over an empty chair:

      forward strokes of earth rich red;
      a kiss of black on the return.

The negative spaces fill themselves.

Today,

my heart left my body
and became a light my soul could follow home

but light can be so difficult
when your brush is tangled up in the stars.

A Need for Broken Things

the sky has stolen something from me
something I should remember

you can almost see it in my eyes,

sun to sea
the dance of a dark slow lament

where, always again,
beauty awaits beyond the momentary dagger;
a recompense of perfect collision;

would there really be beauty without it?

But if I asked you,

if I wrote something so beautiful
your heart stopped
        and your knees felt the weight of
        everything lost

would you stop it all for me?

Jealous lover;
the moon measures my life
in slow wavelengths

our forgiveness is blind

Terns,
      white against forever
place drops of fire into the next fracture
and something I should be holding:

there is nothing reflected in my eyes

White
~for Alba

in the reigning hours

        in the lost hours

banners move December slow
across a canvas quietly forgetting

umber scrawls steal away wingtips full of summer
all along their somnolent distances.

the moon stalks diamonds through branch light

palettes of leaves burn darkly

     drifting

words,
        white as stillness

and the firmament
     just a pale truth past falling.

we have waited lifetimes and reasons,
                       you and I;

lavished here in the lies of every season
as Autumn fires turn cold;

found the silence in shadow realms
lonely in their whispers of sun and sapphire;
watched trees, lonely in their pantomime of
     want and recede
collect light and darknesses

         into places where color waits still:

and your eyes

    your eyes;

  every shade of hungry:

unforgiven
    we'll make a mockery of the waiting

as skies unfurl across pages of unnamed wind
and our hands find heaven in fields of unmade loss

here, where winter strikes softly against white

here; where motion is in everything still

    and heart,
        our only willing hue

A Little Blood to Cover the Dark

The street punk jangles as
he slaps her arm away;
      the dim refrain of
silver chains across studded leather.

A pit bull puppy sits between his Doc Martins;
pushes a Styrofoam container
across the sandy concrete.
He is consumed in his eating;
      unaware that she stares
and draws a slowly hand away.

      Her eyes are settled, but that is all;
      she moves to the twitch of waning alcohol.
A breast spills from her gauze shirt
swollen with waiting life
her end to the
      End of the Road.

A hand drifts to a scab on her forehead,
a reconciliation of remembrance,
recounting something that won't
      return or leave
as if her touch will remove the stain
where the street toughs
push her down onto the pavement
      and take.

Blood is running now.
It helps to cover the dark.

Some things
children should never learn.

Ice Skating

I come here for the coffee,

ice and darkness;
a drown of some comfort.
Alone with the sounds of
ice against the blade;
words rushing by;
shrieks; suddenly and gone;
coaches extol the
virtues of axles and steady
revolutions;
training kids for an event
they will never attend;
deepening the shine
of their often eyes: for naught;
practicing how to be

beautiful.

Corpulent words
are bantered by
self important guardians:

*Meredith's mini-van
dropped the tranny…
fucking American cars!
Coach what's-his-name
is such an asshole!
Can you believe he didn't like
little Danielle's routine?*

These words pass over me;
glacial; reminiscent but
cold…long dead.

They notice me, but
never ask why:

why I sit on the top bleacher;
why I look so often away;
why I talk to myself;

to you.

Help me remember…

this prayer I recite
for all those things
you let slip away with
only a kiss of a promise
you'll write them all
stone down;
they forget their way
back to me now;
the trauma chasing them
so very dark…

lost;

the sounds of your sleep;
there, on the pillow with
the still impression of
your dreaming;
its music and hush;

just there

in the brush of linger
where breath
is only a slight notion
between desires:

unimportant things
that make a home
more than a collection of
preferable debris;

keepsakes of dimly time
that hold me cold
drinking black coffee
here in the quite of ice.

     I hate their fucking coffee.

I huddle against
    my dark;
    my cold;

let my mind axle and revolve;
ice against the blade;
practicing something
I will never again

be.

Essence

if I could know you
across a sky softer than passion;

take the wings from your eyes and set them
into a higher essence of water and light;

trace,
    upturned as forgiveness
the faces that yearn the length of their hours
in prayers,
        silent as touch
for the solace of a more beautiful shadow:

if I could feel quietly your motions
before this fearful stillness stopped our meaning
and collide with you where hearts yet hold fast
and strands of heaven settle down rough as silk;

listen to all the slight notions of darkness
escape through your dreaming

and prostrate myself before
the reticence in each and every sigh
                of your name;

if I could turn away
    in slowly the binding;
reach up through a depth of raven
    that burns softly over me
and loosen the ribbons that won't shine
as bright as the stars they're tangled in

if I could,
        dear God

if I could just unlearn your smile:

hope is for those who don't know how far you can fall

and breath
        for those who no longer care

His Girl

Above the East Fork of
the San Gabriel River
there in the shattered granite
and sifting gold,

a shack fell down
through the slow evening.

The wind,
unhinged in a sway of
Junipers against tired wood
everywhere, left reminders of Buckthorn
and early snow along the canyon rim
as Big Horn walked off into the sky.

I entered through the autumn air
and settled into his memory

       the chair with one good leg
       a table lost mostly to a winter hearth
       cups and plates scattered
       blue enamel beneath the rust
       a lantern repaired with
       a coat hanger and wishes;

       a broken pick left in the broken earth.

A half-empty bottle of Southern Comfort
waited in repose
under a pinup poster
                       his girl
the image held on to color
       in shades of valley fog
except for one spot
worn white against his touch

I took a pull of his bourbon
and wondered how many days he reached for her
as he went out to his work
how long it took to wear away.

I reached for her as I walked through the door.

My hand still felt warm
as I walked away.

3 a.m. connections

as a boy
I remember watching a tug
pulling the rusted bulk of an empty barge against
the strong currents of the upper Columbia River;
the water rushing against the bow made it look
like it was going so very fast when it was nearly
                        standing still

I had never seen anything quite as worn and sad
as that old tug struggling upriver;
in my young eyes it looked a thousand year old
although, these years later I know
the faded lines and days laid down in silent layers of rust
were the result of the labor it did

and I remember later that same day
fishing for young salmon among
the bones and bramble of ancient tugs
where the Columbia empties into the sea;
sleeping away their eternities
in some forgotten corner of the harbor
too tired to make the journey against the current;

torn open for their parts
and bleached the slowest shade of dead
my young eyes had ever seen:

we never start out our journey
to wear away under such useless labor;
       I suppose it just happens

as each wasted lifetime drifts away
in those little tatters of unconnected memory
that startle us awake in the dead hours

when stars fall in those little 2 plus 2's of truth

we only have the courage to embrace
when darkness is perfectly complete

and the heart is too tired
                      too heavy

to long deny

Days Like These
for William Kuechlin

Under his gaze, everything becomes an impossibility.

The hook was a number 10, and my four-year-old fingers were having a tough time getting it to snell. They tangled and re-tangled and dropped in the fluster for the tenth time.

Son! What hell's wrong with you?

Nuthin' Dad...nuthin.

I knew I could do this...I had been practicing all summer. Today was different, though. Much different. The wind turned an impatient oar against the skiff. Mallards laughed their accusatory notions into my panic. I cringed against them. The air droned a buzz under my thoughts. Nothing in my mind was still today.

He was still looking at me...still looking...

Yes!

You did it wrong.
There are only five turns on that snell.
How many do we tie?

Six, Dad.

You're going to lose a fish and cost us dinner.

My first fishing trip. We hadn't caught a thing.

The cork handle of my Zebco 33 was still rough to the touch; too new to be worn smooth in such small hands. I loved that fishing pole. I practiced with it all summer long, and this was my reward: fishing with Dad and Grandpa K on a real boat. I pinned a red worm under the scowl at the stern,

turned my back and read the water
under a deep breath:

Two tree tops sticking out of the water.
Color is darker to the right; deeper water,
Grandpa sez, fish deeper water.

Just like home...

I swung the bait out of my hand and pitched it right into the cover.
Just like pitching the sinker into a paper cup in the
Backyard.

Nothing to it.

Heat was a murky sheen against the blue. The bait faded two feet out of sight...and the reel sang.

ting ting ting ting

A Zebco 33 sounds a little like a wounded school bell when the drag plays out line...and that fish was runnin' freight train away into the weeds.

Don't worry Larry...let him run.
They all come back if you give 'em room.

Grandpa had his hand on my shoulder,
and his eyes on my soul.
He stopped two feet shy of the weeds when I started taking back line.

Held my tongue just so.
Rod tip up...bow to him when he runs.
Take in the line when he stops to rest.
Don't bull him in.

I cranked right up to the surface as he popped out into the sunlight. Glistening teal and gold. Easily a pound; probably more.
Grandpa dropped his hand to my shoulder and gave me a squeeze.

Stupid Bluegill…they taste like crap.
Throw him back and catch a good fish.

I looked at my father just in time to see him turn his back.

I threw my Zebco 33 down, fish, line and all. Teal and gold splashed color onto the grey aluminum hull. It was the only fish we caught that day.

What is wrong with you, Larry?!?

You might wonder how I can remember something that happened when I was only four and a half with such clarity.

Well…no matter how much dark you bury yourself in…or how many bottles you drown yourself in.; no matter how many prayers you say to keep that shadow tucked neatly into a childhood corner;

it just doesn't matter:

days like these never fade.

The journey started out from Escondido. Uncle Max. Old world German. Breakfast of eggs, bratwurst and zwieback. Aunt Susie (pronounced Soooo-sie) she gave you more food than 4 people can eat in one sitting. I can still taste those zwieback biscuits.

Damn.

And my first cup of coffee
very sweet and lots of cream.
Just like Grandpa.
I still drink it just that way.

Laughter and meals
sounds of old world family.
Life and love

the way it was before the wars that drove my family here to the United States. Smiles and happiness my family did not know when they were afraid to admit they were German.

My great grandfather Kuechlin changed the spelling of our name to make it look more American.

He wanted to fit in.

I loved my Uncle Max immediately. Like an older version of my Grandpa K, but with a heavier accent. My Grandpa and Max were natural salesman. Everybody loved them right away; and came back because they were real people, people who loved with abandon, and didn't bother with consequences.

Grandpa…William Kuechlin…Bill, ran the most popular gas station in San Pedro.

A port town; blue collar tough.
People who made their living
with their hands
on the wharfs and in the factories.

Real people living real life.

He ran a Union Oil station; 76. On San Pedro Avenue near Wilmington Avenue, across from Banning High.

It is still there.

Max and Grandpa hugged their brotherhood and laughed their goodbyes as we walked out into the half light of burgeoning day.

We packed into the Ford Fairlane 500 and took off for Lake Henshaw, a mud hole of a lake in the mountains east of San Diego. The road to Henshaw…Highway 78…was a two lane twister through the scrub oak and Manzanita. I sat in the back seat with my thoughts…sliding to and fro on the blood red vinyl; the direction based on the curve and the weight of the foot placed on the Fords pedal.

I thought back to everything I had been taught:

all the lessons my father had given me
and the tips my grandfather had taught me.
I wanted to do this

right.

And I wanted to catch the biggest fish.

In the Kuechlin family, there was no other outcome: we
always catch the biggest fish.

We never go away empty handed. Never.

Nervous talk with Grandpa.
Laughing for no reason.

Singing the old songs
the ones his grandma taught him
German songs of life in the wheat
songs of loving life with old hearts
songs of winters I never knew.

Laughing and laughing

and silly talk between
two hearts connected by life

and the Chevy Bel Air passed us so fast…
the Ford pushed hard to the right.

Around the blind corner;
my eyes can see this

I can see

paper plates billowing
in the perfect morning blue
perfect white against the stone walls

perfect incision of metal and stone

and I can see

I can see

these young eyes
I can see the Ford slowing
see men tumbling blind
see glass and fire
see blood and
see men falling out
see a man holding an eye
back into his head with ruined hands
see a man bleeding from his ears

and

falling

falling

and below
below the man shaking in the dirt
below the flames in morning blue
below the window
below my door
with these young eyes

I see

below the door
the ends of glass and cut

torn cloth

and so much blood

and his face;
turned to meet

his life
his warmth

his memories and meaning

leaving

leaving

leaving him in rhythm with
a heart that refuses to forget.

His eyes were crimson closed by the time his heart
caught up to the memory.

And I was four years to heaven.

We dazed away to call for help.

That's what's wrong, Dad.

    You saw what?

Promise.

No! You did not, son. You did not see that.
Stop it, young man! Quit being stupid.

I saw it too, Larry. I saw him there. We both saw him.

My Father just stared at my Grandpa. He started the boat and
guided it back to the dock. We left for home in silence.

Five days later I jumped off the bus from school and saw a
familiar sight: a teal blue Corvair parked across the street from my
house. I ran in to give my Grandpa a huge hug.

Come on, Larry. I want to take you somewhere. Grab the Zebco.

We drove PCH down to the coast; laughed quietly; my Grandpa teasing me and tickling me and making me laugh. I remember laughing because I never wanted to laugh.

I didn't want to laugh.

We parked in Sunset Beach, near the water tower. Grandpa took me down to the water's edge in Anaheim Bay, and the tide was running in

turning the Eel Grass into the drowning sun
heard the cranes across the long flats
raucous in their meals
heard the splash of fish in the currents.
Heard the Mergansers heading off into night
heard the long call of surf across the shore.
Saw the gold of afternoon
felt it pulling me into quietly black.
Felt the night softly on my eyes.

See him there, Larry...see his fins?
There in the dark water.

I made the cast and caught my first Corbina. Grandpa said he was really big. Took him home for dinner.

We sat in the rushes, there in the breath of darkness
in the light that has forgotten its flame
watched the cranes work into darkness;
whispers of white against deep umber.
You don't forget days like these.
My Grandpa with his arm around me.
A day fading in the hush.

I don't remember going home.

Larry Kuechlin lives and surfs along the Sunset Cliffs in San Diego, California. He has been nominated twice for the Pushcart Prize for Poetry, as well as for the Kate Tufts Discovery Award and the Kingsley Tufts Poetry Award. His literary works include Mountain Biking Orange County with Randy Vogel, Along a Ruined Sea, Along a Ruined Sea, Special Edition, Entrances: 30 Poems and 100 Lines About Love, Elemental, Something Still Visible In the Fire and the Falling Place, along with being published in various periodicals and e-zines. His life is beautifully complicated quite frequently by his two daughters Brandee and Courtney and his persnickety cat, Pogo.

www.ingramcontent.com/pod-product-compliance
Lightning Source LLC
Chambersburg PA
CBHW060750050426
42449CB00008B/1353